Deep Unto Deep

Deep Unto Deep

THE JOURNEY OF HIS EMBRACE

DANA CANDLER

FORERUNNER
PUBLISHING

DEDICATION

To my Matthew

*Truest friend of my heart, my gift of God for the journey—
you are my hero. You love our Beloved God with the whole of
your heart, mind and strength. We wrote this book together. It
was you that sought day after day to make a way for my heart
to voice its song. And as I spent so many hours trying to bring
unspokens into language, you whirled about me with all of
your love as always, taking care of all the natural parts of
life with one hand and holding my heart so lovingly and
brilliantly with the other. I love you*

ACKNOWLEDGEMENTS

Dad and Mom—Who am I without you? Thank you for a lifetime of leading me into intimacy with Jesus and your unwavering zeal for His Name. You are my heroes of the faith.

Deborah—My dear sister and friend since the womb, this is as much your heart on paper as mine. You truly are my sunshine, my messenger of hope and my friend of faith for the journey behind and before.

Dave and Dan—My brothers, my friends, I honor your love and devotion for the One we love, the Man Christ Jesus.

Karli—Your friendship continually compels me back to the place of loving a real Person, back to the simplicity of His heart and mine.

Amybeth—You are my living testimony of the fragrant heart, a life consumed with love wasted on Jesus.

Mike—Thank you for your friendship, your continual sacrifice and your unrelenting wholeheartedness. Most of all thank you for giving your life to 20 year-olds.

CONTENTS

FOREWORD

Across the earth today there is a void of voices calling the Body of Christ into deep intimacy with Jesus. While the vast majority of the church is preoccupied with the latest methods, strategies, and church models, a growing number are pouring their lives into experiencing the Person of Jesus in the place of prayer, Dana being one of them. In *Deep unto Deep*, Dana reminds us of the priceless spiritual principle of holy longing, drawing the human heart into the depths of God's love. Touching the difficult subjects of our barrenness in prayer and the times when God is silent, and exploring the themes of communion with the Holy Spirit and union with God, she addresses the very practical dimensions along with the very mystical dimensions of connecting with God in a life of prayer.

I have had the privilege of knowing Dana and her husband Matt for several years. Both of them are a crucial part of the leadership team at the International House of Prayer since its beginning, in 1999. Over the years I have seen Dana continually choose the "good part" of sitting at the feet of Jesus and cultivating a history of intimacy with Him. His words have formed in her a reality so strong and apparent, and she has unquestionably become a true voice, offering language and keen insight into the heart of Jesus in a way that only experiential understanding can provide. The Lord has gifted Dana with an excellent ability not only to communicate the affections of God, but also to convince and empower the weakest of hearts in their own journeys. She not only proclaims the message of intimacy with clarity and power—she lives the message.

I soberly and gladly recommend *Deep unto Deep* to you as an invaluable resource for your own journey in intimacy with God. The subject matter of deep intimacy with God must not remain merely a vision yet ahead or a hope in the future. Of great importance in this hour of history is for the Church worldwide to become friends of God, which this book is all about. Intimacy with God must grip us today and change the dreams of our hearts—it is our only way forward. I plan on making Dana's book required reading for the International House of Prayer staff as a strategic training tool. I look forward to many more writings from Dana to come about how the human heart connects with God in intimacy!

Mike Bickle, Director of the International House of Prayer of Kansas City

*"Deep calls unto deep at the noise of Your waterfalls;
All Your waves and billows have gone over me"* (Ps. 42:7).

INTRODUCTION

This is a little book about the human heart's journey into the great and glorious deep of God's heart. The question: *How do our weak hearts enter the holy torrents of Divine Love?* For centuries people have written on this subject, and I do not aspire to write beyond their accounts. In fact, my desire is to write beneath them— to speak in simple words and in a slow manner—for I find my own heart to be simple and slow and in need of this manner of application.

There is a cry in each one of us for what is real...for touching the very substance of our existence and drinking deeply of the Man who calls Himself, "Living Water," the One from whom all purpose and meaning proceeds. Yet in the narrow universe between our own hearts and the heart of the living God, we encounter a painful and disorienting breach. In our times of prayer, we find mostly silence, emptiness and barrenness. We, of course, perceive these effects to be utterly not of God and only proof of our own failure. We have yet to discover the jewels He has hidden within these arid contributors to the journey. And thus, in our pursuit, we have become discouraged in the very thing we were made for: *intimacy with the Son of God.*

Surely there is a Man behind the pages of the Word of God. A very real Man sits upon a very real throne behind the veil of this life on the earth. Surely there is Someone *real* that my prayers reach when I lift my voice. That Person, that Man, I can quote many a line from and tell many a story of. Even at times, I can pray many a prayer to. But what within that is true relationship? Where is my human heart truly touching and connecting with the Divine Heart of God? What is rhetoric and what is real? When I stand before Him face to face one day soon, when I meet His eyes for the first time, will I experience a memory in that gaze? Will there be familiarity? Will the intimacy that I have known with Him in this life of earth resound with real substance through the corridors of Eternity? Will I *know* Him?

My question is this: how do we move from knowing about this Man Jesus, whom we love, into that longed for place of knowing Him intimately? How do our hearts move from the place of looking from a distance at the God of the Word to intimately experiencing the fullness of intimacy with Him?

Along with this cry for intimacy comes the urgency of its necessity. Present tense intimacy with the Lamb of God is so necessary for the hour in which we are living. In our day, the tensions and fears steadily rise across the earth. Together as a generation, we will face the greatest glory the human heart has ever beheld, along with the greatest pressures the world has ever known. Only one thing will equip and sustain our hearts for what lies ahead: intimacy with God. It is the personal knowing of the heart of our Beloved God and the inward communion with His Holy Spirit. A cry is going out across the globe for what is real, for the knowledge of God in its raw form. Who has been with Him? Who knows His heart? Who has actually lived in His presence? This cry is for those who have been in the counsel of the Lord, who have discerned His heart and known His embrace (Jer. 23:18). Yet in this time of crises there is a famine in the land of *true reality and intimacy* with God.

The cry going out across the body of Christ in our day is a request as ancient as humanity and as needed as the air we breathe. It is the desire for the kind of intimacy with the living God that Jesus described the wise virgins as knowing (Matt. 25:1-13). It is the desire to know and be known—to feel and to experience the One in Whom all life flows. It is a cry of desperation for inward lamps found burning at Christ's return. In the hearts of believers all across the earth, this groan is increasing. The ache is intensifying. We have grown tired of words and bored with ideas. We are weary of hearing of a God of love and not experiencing the power of His affections. We are burdened with stories about times that He came and our own lack of experience of His presence. We want a living flame within. We do not want only a theology about the experience of God but the true encounter with Jesus Christ from which the theology is birthed. We do not want only concepts, but the relationship with Him that infuses the concepts with living breath. We do not want to only hear about Jesus, we want to know Him, to touch Him and to find His embrace. We want reality.

It is right that this deep ache for reality would be our cry. It is not as though this burning originated with our own affections or was cultivated through our own goodness. No, the Lord Himself has entrusted this kindled flame to our desirous hearts, and He is the One who tends to its burnings. He alone can bring the ache into the place of ultimate satisfaction. Our hunger for Him is a supernatural awakening, and His answer is a divine enflaming. He has given us this ache so that He might answer it. He has caused our souls to hunger so that, in time, they might be fed by Himself alone. He has placed within us this urgency so that at the midnight hour, bright shining lamps, filled with the oil of intimacy, might arise from the darkness and bring light to many. This pursuit from awakening to enflaming is indeed the journey of His embrace.

God has arranged our earthly lives so that our intimacy with Him is cultivated through the seasons of our journey. My question has been: what insights has the Lord given us to shed light into this holy pursuit? How is this journey revealed? We have been given the help of the Word, namely the Song of Songs, and the portrayal of the body of Christ's way as a cherished bride. We have been given the Helper, the Holy Spirit, to ever lead us and guide us into greater love as we journey forward. And we have been given each other— saints of God past and present and the testimonies held within the experience of each one. Together with these escorts, we endeavor to paint the portrait, to add one color here and another there, to reveal the many shades of God's palate and bring to light the purpose of God in this mysterious process of romance between God and the human soul.

This text, including real journal-entry prayers and heart-crys from my own journey, is my contribution to the masterpiece that the Holy Spirit is unfolding about the journey unto the deep of Love, comprised of so many seasons and filled with so much diversity. It is important to mention that, though these seasons have a certain flow, they are not of the kind of movement that can be divided and aligned in a step-by-step progression. As lovers on this pilgrimage, we are not climbing a generic staircase where we graduate from one point to the next until we finally reach the place of love's fullness. Rather, each season is handcrafted by the Bridegroom God for the very specific heart He enwraps within it. And the progression of each lover's way is a perfect weaving, designed by utter brilliance, wisdom and love. Though one season may follow suite with the descriptions later given, another will break every rule just as a snowstorm in spring. As diverse as each person is each one's journey, and we can form no common method of steps or stages to measure our way forward. For the moment we think we have graduated from one place, we are rushed backward to what we presumed to be three steps before it. Indeed, we will waste much emotional energy to measure our way. Rather, let us peer with wonder into the mystery of the complexity of each small part of the pilgrimage. Let us grow in love not by departmentalizing but by ever-increasing in sheer marvel at the intimacy portrayed by the detail of each season along the way.

"A Prayer of Barrenness"

My heart aches. I love Him, yes, but faintly.
I desire Him, yes, but weakly.
I want Him, true, but waveringly.
Even the pain that lies within
I recognize to be such faint pain,
A mere discomfort next to the heart-wrenching anguish
That grips true lovers
My knowledge is nothing. My wisdom, infancy.
I see nothing as it truly is.
Eternity what is light. This life of earth what is dark.
Stories remain stories. Not sinking deep within my soul,
And scarring me with Divine invasion
Your cross is a picture, Your Heaven a fantasy.
Tears are sweet emotions, moved by Your sacrifice.
But not the tears of sharing in Your sufferings.
I say Your name so sweetly but do not know its Face.
All I am is far. So distant, so removed.
But You beckon me come.
Yet, my Lord, I am nothing. I have nothing. I know nothing.
When I thought I had something,
It dissolved before Your beauty,
And I was left naked. Possessing nothing.
Poor for words. Empty of all. Needy and alone.
Even so, my Love, call me.
Yes, do not leave me here but beckon me come.
Though I have nothing, though I am only poor,
I cast myself on your unfailing love
Where else would I go?
Whom have I but You?

Chapter 1

The Nobility of Barren Prayer

I remember the day so clearly. Actually, I remember plenty of them and even still experience my fair share of them. What long and empty collections of hours in prayer they include. Days of barren prayer. I remember one day very specifically that, in truth, was not too unlike most of the others. It was not the first day of its kind but one of the harder days, to be sure. More than anything, I desired communion with God and to be rid of the internal compulsions that hindered the fellowship that I was made for. I wanted my Lord to catch the little foxes ever nipping at the vines within my heart (Song Sol. 2:15). I knew that this would transpire only in sitting in the place of my barrenness before the One that I loved, replacing the invitations of secondary comforts with the One Compulsion who is worthy, the Magnificent Obsession of all the ages. Only *there* would all of my false clingings surrender their hold.

Alone in my room. Bible open. Schedule cleared. Heart expectant. And only quiet to meet me. Only silence to accompany me. My words seemed to drop to the ground. The pages of my journal were empty. There were no tears to offer in longing. Prayer was hard. The Word was not moving nor causing my heart to be tenderized. All emotions seemed to sleep. One hour turned to two as I watched the clock almost minute by minute. This was one of the days when I could hardly remember the point of my focus. Why was I here? What was I doing? What was the point of the waiting? Have I missed it entirely? Is this all a waste? I moved from sitting to pacing, from reading to praying quietly and from praying quietly to silence. Still nothing. No response. No movement. No sound. Two hours turned to three. Morning turned to afternoon. And on and on the day went—slowly and painfully empty—the day of a waiting heart in barren prayer.

Though the story might seem better if I now expressed a turning point when all of the sudden God broke in and everything changed, it did not. For that is neither the true story nor the point of its illustration. Afternoon turned to evening, and I found myself in my car driving aimlessly. Parking in a shopping area parking lot, away from the other cars, I watched the people come and go so casually, all the while still lifting my heart in prayer to God. I looked through my windshield to the sky of clouds and felt the distance between my own heart and the Creator of the earth. Finally finding tears, I cried in pain, not in sweetness, "O God, when will You come to my little heart?"

"I CAN THINK OF NO MORE NOBLE WAY TO SPEND A DAY THAN TO SPEND IT WITH YOU, WHETHER I FEEL YOUR NEARNESS OR NOT."

Ending my day that night, so relieved to see its completion, I could only say one last thing to the Lord: *"Write it down in our book, O God. Though it was so empty and so dry, may it count in an eternal relevance I do not yet comprehend. Write it down so that one day You might read to me of its preciousness. Remember this day, though I know it will blend into so many days just like it in my own memory. Count it as valuable to the heart of God. And O God, give me one grace, I pray. Give me the grace to give myself in prayer once again tomorrow. To believe that it matters. To put my heart before You though I feel so unproductive and unfruitful. Give me the grace to spend tomorrow once more before You in love. For I can think of no more noble way to spend a day than to spend it with You, whether I feel Your nearness or not. Oh, help me in the times of fainting. Give me the grace for one more day."*

The Richness of What We Call Barrenness

"'Sing O barren, you who have not borne! Break forth into singing, and cry aloud, you who have not labored with child! For more are the children of the desolate than the children of the married woman,' says the Lord" (Is. 54:1).

We are on a journey into the heart of God, and that journey is essentially one of prayer and communion with the One we love. As we position ourselves to know this fellowship with God, coming before Him in devotion and prayer, one of the very hardest and most common things that we encounter are the times of emptiness we experience. When we come before Him, we hope for times of exhilaration, yet instead we find ourselves watching the clock for when the hour will be through. Instead of tears, we feel barrenness. We sit in

our rooms or in our place of prayer, and we wait. We
read the Word, saying it back to Him in prayer. We pace.

*HE HAS
COMPOSED OUR
JOURNEY TO
NOT ONLY
INCLUDE TIMES
RICH WITH
SOUND AND
EMOTION BUT
ALSO ALL THE
TIMES OF
EMOTIONLESS
QUIET AND
STILLNESS.*

We sing. We watch. We lift our voice.
We lift our hearts. And we feel
nothing. We see nothing. In all natural
considerations, nothing is happening.
We don't hear Him. We don't feel
Him. We can't tangibly behold anything that He is doing in our hearts.
We spend long hours in an empty
room with no response from heaven
and no experience of God. It is
enough to greatly discourage and
even keep us from this whole pursuit
of Him, unless we understand what is
transpiring in His heart in these
times. We have to know what His
heart is like and just what He feels in these seemingly
barren days.

The testimony of these prayers from the Eternal
Eyes is that *they matter*. They indescribably count in the
ascent up the mountain of the knowledge of God. They
are the pages that fill the book. They are the normal
days between the extremes. And He has designed them
to be so. He has composed our journey to not only
include times rich with sound and emotion but also all
the times of emotionless quiet and stillness. They, too,
are part of the journey. These times *feel* barren to us,
but they are not. They are far from fruitless to the
Ancient of Days, and He does not forget one moment
of their composition. Soon we shall reap a harvest for

if we sow to the Spirit, surely we will reap of the Spirit (Gal. 6:8).

The Lord does not despise our weakness as we so often imagine. He is not caught off-guard by our frailty. Quite the contrary, as Creator and Savior, He loves and enjoys the process of our finding our strength in Him and learning to lean into Him. It is in our weakness that His strength is made perfect (2 Cor. 12:9), and it is out of weakness that we are made strong (Heb. 11:34). He has set up His kingdom with the inclusion of our weakness. "For though He was crucified in weakness, yet He lives by the power of God. For we also are weak in Him, but we shall live with Him by the power of God..." (2 Cor. 13:4). He is not a High Priest who cannot sympathize with us in this weakness (Heb. 4:15). He knows it fully and embraces us in this place as He beckons us to continually lift our weak voice and our weak gaze in prayer and communion with Him.

In these times of such weakness and barrenness, the grace that God imparts to our hearts is the grace of the "one more day." One of the small but not insignificant graces we find as we arise in the morning is the strength to pursue Him with eyes of faith for one more day. These long days of barren prayer hold but one light at the end of their darkened tunnels: their completion. We reach our beds at the close of these days as the single victory worth recording. We made it. Though faint and weak and disillusioned, we said, "Yes." Our one prayer cast toward heaven is that somehow He will call these feeble fumblings valuable and that with His matchless wisdom He would redefine these seemingly stationary seasons as essential movements on the journey.

The Lord invites the one who is barren—the one who has not yet known what it is to bear fruit and reap the harvest of labor—to lift her voice and sing (Isaiah 54:1). He reveals how deeply He values this song though it arises from the midst of emptiness. Prayers lifted to the Lord and songs sung to Him from our place of dryness are desired by Him. He is not waiting for us to bear fruit and experience what we would call "victory" in prayer before we lift our voice.

HE CALLS IT A VICTORY WHEN WE WILLINGLY LIFT OUR VOICE TO HIM FROM THE WILDERNESS OF OUR BARRENNESS. THIS HE CALLS NOBLE.

He calls it a victory when we willingly lift our voice to Him from the wilderness of our barrenness. This He calls noble. This He deems wise. In this place, our weak words overcome His great heart.

The Wisdom of the Waiting

So often in these times of barren prayer, the accusation that arises is that we are doing it wrong. Our math tells us that if we were doing it right, He would come, and we would experience more of God. The dry emptiness confirms to us that we must have missed it. For everyone else, it either must have come naturally or the formula must have been given to them by God, telling them how to meet Him in prayer. We wonder if we should change what we are praying or the passage we are reading in the Word. We consider that perhaps our method of prayer is wrong or that we should find a new approach. Maybe *then* He will come.

The cry arises from our hearts, "Where are You God?" Nothing moves. No one speaks. Only quiet. Only silence. Today looks just like yesterday, empty and ordinary. We know for sure that nothing is happening on the outside, and the ever-lurking accusation is that neither is anything happening within. It seems that all the energy of our culture and history comes against us at a rapid speed to convince us of the wastefulness of waiting before our God. We think, "It may have been right for Daniel or for Mary or David, but they obviously knew something I do not know. Or God gave them a grace that He did not give to me. Or they lived in a time of a greater anointing of God, and He does not manifest Himself now in the way He did then." All of these thoughts and so many more race about our minds as we sit there in quiet, hanging on for dear life. This is the time that we must wage the warfare of faith, reminding our souls how significant these weak days are to Him and just how wise He deems them. "But without faith it is impossible to please Him, for he who comes to God must believe that He is, and that He is a rewarder of those who diligently seek Him" (Heb. 11:6).

The God Who is Overcome

In Song of Solomon 4:9, our Beloved Jesus speaks to us and says, "You have ravished my heart, my sister, my spouse. You have ravished my heart with one look of your eyes, with one link of your necklace." He gives insight into what transpires in His own heart with every weak glance that we lift to Him and with every small choice of our will to love Him. So many of these weak glances and small choices are made in the place of dryness, when we feel nothing. God does not define our love by emotion as we so often do. We love to measure our experience of God by what is felt. Love cannot be evaluated with this system of calculation. God is the One who measures love and what we call barren He often calls fruitful; what we call wasteful He often calls well spent. He "… calls those things which do not exist as though they did…" (Rom. 4:17).

In our weak devotion, He is ravished over us. So unthinkable the words yet true, nonetheless. The earth is the Lord's and the fullness thereof, yet He has committed the affections of His heart to be overcome by the likes of you and me. Weak, fainthearted, prone-to-discouragement hearts of men. He has angels without number, and He knows each star by name, yet by my small heart, He is conquered. No army could overcome this mighty One. The kings of the earth take their stand against Him, and He laughs with divine amusement (Ps. 2:4). Yet there is one thing, shall I say figuratively, one "weak spot" in His heart. He has allowed one arrow to successfully pierce His mighty heart—the arrow from a believer on the earth who gives Him the weak glance of a lovesick heart. It is the small choice of a voluntary heart to love Him though it cannot see Him.

HE HAS ALLOWED ONE ARROW TO SUCCESSFULLY PIERCE HIS MIGHTY HEART—THE WEAK GLANCE OF A LOVESICK HEART.

We stand on our tiptoes on the precipice of time, peering into eternity with a steady gaze, ever searching the horizon for the One who lives outside of time. We peer into a mystery, and the glass that we look through is darkened and dim (2 Cor. 3:18). Having not seen Him, we love Him (1 Pet. 1:8), and so with a gaze reaching for a world unseen, we look to our Beloved in prayer. It is this gaze that overcomes Him and sends Him into this whirlwind of poetic song, "Turn your eyes away from me! For they have overcome me!" (Song Sol. 6:5). I imagine Jesus, with eyes as flames of fire, turning to His Father and exclaiming, *"Look at her Father! She has not seen Me yet she believes! She is once more lifting her eyes to Me. She has chosen to fix her gaze again upon what is unseen. Oh, she overcomes Me! How she conquers My heart with her lovesick gaze!"*

This is what is happening in the spirit while we struggle to believe on the earth. We lift up our weak faith as we come to Him in prayer. We choose again and again to believe that He cherishes our feeble words and holds each sigh close to His heart. At the end of the day, after we have experienced what feels like nothing, we return to our beds and say with hearts of faith, "It counts, doesn't it? I'm storing up something, aren't I? These tears that no one else sees except You, You will show me one day, won't You?" And we believe for one more day. We reach into the unseen. And though we feel the constant possibility that we could have just wasted today in prayer, we choose to believe that He sees differently. What we feel is worth forgetting, He holds as precious in His remembrance. One day He will say, "It counts! It counts! Everything counted! It was all a part of My perfect plan. You came into agreement with something you could not even see or reach. And every movement of your heart, every choice of your will toward Me holds eternal worth!"

I believe these faint movements of my heart, made in the times of such grey shadows, move His heart like no other time. The times—when I feel nothing yet choose to believe in His heart and His love—these undo the heart of the God of Heaven. On the days when every accusation lurks over my head and all the voices of condemnation join forces against me, my weak heart overcomes Him as I choose to believe what presently seems an absurdity—that God is for me and that my prayer, though weak, is wisdom. These are the days He holds precious. Oh how they move His heart. I believe more than the days when we feel so much, when all is clear and when hope is so near. These barren days are called precious by the Lord. "Blessed are those who have not seen and yet believed" (Jn. 20: 29).

THE TIMES— WHEN I FEEL NOTHING YET CHOOSE TO BELIEVE IN HIS HEART AND HIS LOVE—THESE UNDO THE HEART OF THE GOD OF HEAVEN.

Each choice He records; each glance He remembers. And one very real day in our future, He will open up the book of remembrance and remind us of each one. He will say, "Do you remember this time? You were so discouraged, so disheartened, so desperate. Yet you chose once again to believe in Me and to receive My love. You said, 'Yes,' to Me though you could neither feel nor see Me."

I Will Remember Your Love

The Song of Solomon begins with the cry of the bride and her companions saying, "We will remember your love more than wine" (Song Sol.1:4). She vows to remember His affections throughout her journey and in her darkest nights to meditate on the love He has revealed to her in times past. This is her commitment to Him. It is a beautiful and necessary vow she offers. Yet I believe it is only an echo of a greater promise—the promise of the Lord Himself. He says to our fainting hearts as we come to Him time and time again with weak prayers lifted high, "I will remember your love, my sister, my bride. You have vowed to Me that you will remember My love, but I say to you, I will remember your love for all eternity. I will reveal the relevance of all the weak moments of faith that you yourself have long forgotten and My Father who sees in secret will reward you openly (Matt. 6:6). I will declare to all the heavenly hosts the true weightiness of the prayers you considered so weak when you offered them. *I will remember your love.*"

He will remember our tears. One day, He will wipe each one away forever. And I believe this is why He keeps them in a bottle (Ps. 56:8). They are indescribably precious to Him. We only have one life on the earth to cry them, and then forever they are the treasures of our intimacy's history. Though their lifespan is temporal and not eternal, they are the testimonies of our existence on the earth. Every tear cried in love will be remembered. *"...And the Lord God will wipe away tears from all faces; the rebuke of His people He will take away from all the earth; for the Lord has spoken. And it will be said in that day: 'Behold this is our God; we have waited for Him, and He will save us. This is the Lord; we have waited for Him; we will be glad and rejoice in His salvation'"* (Is. 25:8-9). Every movement of the heart toward Him in the midst of hardship will be trumpeted forever. The Father who sees what is done in secret will reward us openly (Matt. 6:6). The divine exchange is that we "remember His love" in our seasons on the earth, and then for all eternity He will remember our love.

And yes, I believe that He will bring to us a very real bottle containing the tears that we have cried. Not one will be lost. Not one will be forgotten. He will know each one by name and the story that it comprises. One by one, He will remind us of the movements of our hearts in the age when we could but see so dimly. He will tear by tear remember our love, remembering what we have long forgotten and bringing nobility forever to the moments of barren prayer and lovesick heartache that we had thought so weak.

The Nobility of the Journey's Entirety

To know that each small choice matters and that every tear holds eternal significance within the heart of the Lamb of God changes everything for us and enables us to give ourselves unreservedly to the journey of the heart. We begin to recognize eternity hiding in the shadows of each feeble prayer and every small movement of our hearts toward the Lord. Beyond that, we find the same everlasting weight and worth within the borders of every season in our spiritual life. In giving ourselves to lives of prayer, our prayers will not all feel barren in our experience. Yet neither will they all be saturated with presence and the experience of communion. The important thing we must learn is that no matter what we encounter along the way, we must find the intimacy provided in that place. We must discern the significance of each step along the way. In every moment of the day and in each season of the journey, we can know that therein is hidden an invitation from the One we love. He forever and always provides for us an open door into greater love. We have a Bridegroom God who is after the fullness of fellowship in our lives. If we will but give Him our agreement, He will give us opportunity to go deeper and deeper into the love of God until the day we see His face. We are never without an avenue into greater love. Every heart in every place along the way can know that wherever he stands, whether valley or mountaintop or somewhere in between, a doorway of greater intimacy is before him.

Perhaps the greatest beginning point to understanding the intimacy to be found in each season is the very reference point of all creation, the God-Man Jesus Christ who is forever our eternal Bridegroom. In finding out the movements of His great heart, we have a compass for our own journey. In plunging the deep of His Person, we begin to partake of that which will sustain us and exhilarate us for all the ages to come. We will find that truly our journey has only just begun...

"Tears"

Storms around me...my heart is pulled from side to side. Small things seem big to my little heart...but I fix my eyes on You. Be my strength this night, Jesus. For You are my rock and my strong *tower. You are my shelter and my hiding place. If You are for me, who can be against me? There is <u>nothing</u>. Neither death, nor life, nor angels, nor principalities, nor things present, nor things to come, nor powers, nor height, nor depth, nor any other created thing that shall be able to separate me from the love of God, which is in Christ Jesus, our Lord (Rom. 8:38). Nothing. You have declared my heart Yours. Oh restful thought that my heart belongs to You. If God be jealous for my heart, who can stand in His way.*

> *Jesus...one day soon I will not remember these tears. This night will fade from memory and blend into a hundred other nights so similar. With it will fade the pain in my heart. But You will not forget. You will remember. Every tear has its own story with You. You keep each one in Your bottle. You know every thought and emotion that caused each one. Oh, who is He who loves me so by remembering forever each one of my tears? So tonight, though I cannot even say why I cry so, I offer each tear to You. For the bottle, Jesus. For the book. Keep them. Keep every one. And one day, tell me the story again.*

"Jealous Love"

Little mountain, what are you?
Little ocean, where lies your strength?
If the Hand that formed the universe holds my heart,
How can man or power take me from Him?
His love leaves the oceans small
And the mountains powerless to separate.
The One that loves me
Will not surrender me to another hand
Though all of hell stands in His way.
He will have me. He will keep me.
He will not give me over to any other.
I had thought that I could lose my way
Until I remembered jealousy keeps me.
He keeps me,
And I'm a fool to think another could steal
What He has called His own.
If the Consuming Fire is ravished by my small heart,
What man of the earth,
What power of heaven or hell,
Can keep me from Him?
No mountain He would not conquer;
No sea He would not cross.
Foolish I was to fear that all could be lost.
My heart is not kept by my own love,
But by the River of love from His heart.
I am my Beloved's and He is mine.

CHAPTER 2

HE IS A BRIDEGROOM

"You have ravished my heart, my sister, my spouse; You have ravished my heart with one look of your eyes..." (Song Sol. 4:9).

The heart of God is ravished with enjoyment and delight over His people. We cannot pass by this quickly. We have known the concept of His love, yes, but often this very knowing and familiarity is what hinders us from ever entering into the depths and actually drinking from the deep wells of Love's plentitude. We cannot let common words stand-in for experienced realities. To say that He loves me is a familiar notion indeed, but to pursue, know and experience His love is a rare preoccupation. Our familiarity with the words deceives us into thinking we have personally known the exceedingly vast riches that lie beyond the realm of language and in the eternal deep of God's heart. We confuse the hearing of a concept with the actual abiding of that reality inside of us. Yet His Love is a realm that transcends all mental comprehension and leaves all utterance ashamedly barren. It is to this unknown world of eternal pleasures that we give ourselves as we begin our pilgrimage into His ravished heart.

God describes His Love in the Word *as surpassing knowledge* (Eph 3:19). Paul proclaims, "'...Eye has not seen, nor ear heard, nor have entered into the heart of man the things which God has prepared for those who love Him"' (1 Cor. 2:9). A raging River of affections surges within His heart. It is a holy, violent flow of love. Daniel beheld a fiery stream coming forth from before the throne of the Ancient of Days. In Psalm 36, David describes a glorious river of pleasures, the very fountain of life that God causes His people to drink from. This river of desire within His heart is the one route into the place of intimacy that we long for. We can hear a thousand teachings and read a hundred books, but we will only find the satisfaction of our search in the deep of His heart. We must plunge the Person of Jesus Christ. It is not casually or from a distance that we dive into the depths of these vast regions, but rather we enter this Ocean by a focused abandonment, a violent pursuit and a lifelong drinking.

We were made for this love. Our entire story is wrapped up within its tale. For love we were created, and in love is our eternal testimony. It is our reason, our purpose, our end and our beginning. We have heard with our ears of a God of love, and we have known

> WE HAVE HEARD WITH OUR EARS OF A GOD OF LOVE, AND WE HAVE KNOWN WITH OUR MINDS THAT IN THIS LOVE IS OUR LIFE, BUT HAVE WE YET BEEN EMBRACED BY LOVE HIMSELF?

with our minds that in this love is our life, but have we yet been embraced by Love Himself? Have we deeply considered love's mysterious nature that has caused the entire purpose of mankind to be a stunning narrative of holy romance? Have we been overcome with delight and wonder at the boldness of Love's pursuit? Indeed, we have not yet even begun to search its treasuries. Language we have, perhaps, but the living glories of Love's delights we have only just begun to peer into. Though love is our eternal story, we do not yet even slightly recognize or know it. This is the journey we are embarking upon. It is the voyage into Love Himself.

The Everlasting Story

To begin the great story of our existence we must start at the end. For the end of natural history best unveils the beginning and all that lies between. The end of our story, as recorded in Revelation 19, is *a glorious wedding day.* This passage magnificently announces the ultimate purpose of all creation and the natural order. It reveals the day when the bride of Christ meets her heavenly Bridegroom and the marriage covenant is established.

In this passage, we find a great multitude gathered together on the sea of glass like crystal. The Body of Christ, all the saints from all history, will finally be assembled together for the first time. An anticipation that has been building for thousands of years will fill the air as each person looks around in wonder, beholding with natural eyes for the first time what he or she had only ever peered into with eyes of faith. Our voice of one will sound from the throne of God, saying,

"Praise our God, all you His servants and those who fear Him, both small and great!" God will fling wide the great door of invitation and beckon believers to release the song of their heart to Jesus, the Desire of All Nations! Together, we will ascribe our love and declare our affections to the One who is beautiful and glorious!

This wondrous end of natural history was purposed from before there was time. In the mysteries of eternity past, God the Father, God the Son and the Holy Spirit dwelled in unsurpassed union and intimacy. The Holy Three have always existed as a divine dance of romance, a whirlwind of affection and pleasure and love unending. It was from this pulsating intimacy that God created humanity and the natural order. Though we will always remain the creation, He formed humanity to enter into relationship with the Trinity, the Godhead. In His great mysterious heart was a desire to bring human beings into the holy river of affections known between Father, Son and Holy Spirit, and to share in this Divine communion with them. The Father desired a family, and the Son desired a bride. From this overflow of burning desire, humanity was brought forth.

Yet it was not without a determined price established before creation that this glorious union would come to pass. It was for this ultimate end and purpose of eternal intimacy between God and man that the Lamb was slain before the foundations of the world (Rev. 13:8). To bring humanity into this astounding position of nearness with Himself, Jesus was crucified, and we were hidden in Him (Col. 3:3). It was for the joy set before Him, His eternal inheritance promised Him by His Father, that He endured the cross. He had the power to lay down His life and the power to take it up again, and He laid it down by His own choosing (John 10:18). Taking upon Himself our punishment, we are clothed in the very righteousness of Christ, justified freely by His grace and given eternal peace with God. For He chose us in Him before the foundation of the world, that we might be holy and blameless before Him in love, forever *accepted in the* Beloved (Eph. 1:6).

When God created Adam, He said to him, *"I will make a partner suitable to you."* The Holy Spirit revealed to Paul that this promise ultimately speaks of Jesus and the church (Eph. 5:32). When God said this to Adam, He was declaring the hidden purpose of His heart from eternity past, the mystery of

> *HE DESIRED TO BRING FORTH VOLUNTARY LOVERS OF GOD, ENTIRELY POSSESSED BY JESUS...*

the ages, to bring forth for His Son His own bride that would be a fitting and suitable companion. He desired to bring forth voluntary lovers of God, entirely possessed by Jesus, a people who chose Him and lived out of the spontaneous overflow of their hearts rather than by mandatory obedience. The Father has kept this eternal motivation central in His administration and unfolding of all human history. He planned the wedding day, this unprecedented celebration feast, so that we, the dust of the earth, redeemed by the blood of Jesus, could end natural history where we began—in the embrace of the Son of God.

On that final day, Jesus *will* have affectionate partners who are voluntary lovers fully possessed by Him, and natural history will culminate with a lovesick bride in the image of Jesus, ruling the Kingdom of God with Him! "'Then the kingdom and dominion, and the greatness of the kingdoms under the whole heaven, shall be given to the people, the saints of the Most High...'" (Dan. 7:27). Oh how great is the mystery, this hidden plan that God has designed from before the ages!!

Bridegroom Heart

"...And as the bridegroom rejoices over the bride, so shall your God rejoice over you" (Is. 62:5).

There is One seated upon the throne high above the circle of the earth. The Nations are His inheritance (Ps. 2:8). One day every knee will bow and confess Lordship to this Worthy Man (Rom. 14:11). Yet there is more to this Man Jesus than His governmental lordship and His transcendent majesty. There is more than His position as King and His supremacy as Lord. It is what lives within His great heart. The One who is fully God and fully Man possesses fierce burning love and jealously desires each of our hearts individually. He pursues each one of us with intimate understanding and personal affection. We have received Him as Savior, understood Him as Brother and known Him as Shepherd. He is King. He is Lord. He is Master. Yet the revelation moving rapidly toward our distant hearts is that He is also our eternal Bridegroom.

"'And it shall be, in that day,' says the Lord, 'That you will call Me "My Husband," and no longer call Me "My Master"'" (Hosea 2:16). For all of time God has been unfolding who He is to humanity. He has been progressively revealing and emphasizing new faces of His personality and aspects of His character. As history has moved forward generation by generation, it is as though He has said, "Now I will open this window of My personality, and now I will unlock this door of My being." When God opens a window of who He is to the body of Christ, what He has already spoken and revealed of Himself in His Word becomes alive and experienced by believers in a corporate dimension.

The final revelation of Himself that God will cause to be known and experienced in a corporate way by the body of Christ is that of a Bridegroom. Never in history has the entire body of Christ held this revelation of God's heart in a central and dominant position. Yet even now the Holy Spirit is awakening hearts everywhere to this understanding of Jesus. He is beginning to cause believers to know Him as the Lover of their souls. Truly, He has saved the best for last in that we will finally know Him as Husband instead of Master. Our Master is becoming our Lover.

Jesus, fairer than all of the sons of men, with the abundance of grace poured upon His lips, is the One who is anointed by His Father with the *oil of gladness* above all His companions (Ps. 45:2, 7). The One who is the most beautiful and the richest in grace is also the *happiest* Man in all of heaven and earth. He rejoices over us with gladness and singing (Zeph. 3:17). His heart overflows with enjoyment and delight. Many times in scripture God speaks of the actual fact of His joy, but only once, in Isaiah 62:5, does He actually elaborate on what *kind* of joy it is that dwells within Him. He says,

"My delight over you is like a Bridegroom rejoicing over his bride."

Jesus' last public message to the human race before He went to the cross was a message of a Bridegroom. He said, "'The kingdom of heaven is like a certain king who arranged a marriage for his son...'" (Matt. 22:1). It was His only public declaration of the Bridegroom revelation and the only time in His earthly ministry that He called the bride to Himself with His own lips. The final cry of Jesus, the one He waited until the very last precious moments of His earthly ministry to release, was for a bride. His final message was an invitation to bridal partnership, the great plan of the ages. Right before He endured the cross, He stood as a Bridegroom giving this invitation to bridal intimacy.

Moments before He went through the darkened doorway of Gethsemane, He lifted His eyes to heaven in the high priestly prayer to His Father. In John 17:24, He said, "'Father, I desire that they also whom You gave Me may be with Me where I am, that they would behold My glory." As the burning heart of the Eternal Bridegroom faced the cross and the greatest agony His heart would ever know, His volcanic emotions erupted, and He cried out His desire to His Father. He voiced His longing for those He loves to be with Him where He is. He willed that they would behold and enter into the experience of the glory that His Father gave Him before the foundation of the world.

As His natural eyes were set like flint toward Golgotha, the eyes of His spirit saw something far beyond the anguish of the cross and the silencing of the tomb. He looked all the way through the corridors of time to the final horizon of the natural order. There His gaze locked on the glorious marriage that awaited Him, and this indescribable joy set before Him empowered His heart to drink the cup of suffering His Father commanded Him.

These same eyes that looked toward the great wedding day while yet on the earth are described in Revelation 19:12 as eyes like a flame of fire. At the very center of His personality, He is aflame with Love. One of the first revelations that God gave of Himself in the Word is that of a Consuming Fire. He says in Deut. 4:24, "For the LORD your God is a consuming fire, a jealous God." He said in essence, "Know this of Me first: My whole being is ablaze with fire." He gave this resemblance to portray His passion and jealous emotions for His people. Fire was one of the only legitimate descriptions to describe the jealous nature of His love.

THE ONE WHO IS THE HAPPIEST MAN ALIVE IS ALSO THE ALL CONSUMING FIRE...

The One who is the happiest Man alive is also the All Consuming Fire; His joy and His jealousy hold no contradiction. He fiercely desires that nothing would come between Him and His bride. Out of passionate desire, He zealously destroys all that hinders and stands in the way of love. His fire consumes the heart of His bride with love. When He gazes into her eyes, the very fire of His gaze imparts and protects the supernatural love flowing within her heart. He describes His love in the Song of Solomon with unmatched description. "...Love is as strong as death, jealousy as cruel as the grave; its flames are flames of fire, a most vehement flame. Many waters cannot quench love, nor can the floods drown it" (Song Sol. 8:6-7).

When we encounter this unyielding love, this love so jealous that no power on the earth can prevail against it, a fierce peace embraces our trembling hearts. It is His jealousy that keeps us. It is His zeal that sustains us on our way and makes us to walk on our high places (Hab. 3:19). The Father in His zeal for His Son will bring forth a worthy bride. The Son in His ardent love for His Father will present us to Him as a holy people, the family of God. The Holy Spirit in His devotion to the Son will equip us and accomplish His way within us. The great arm of the Lord and all of the might of heaven uphold the force of this love. Lest we think that we ourselves keep our own hearts, we must rest assured in God's own zeal to bring our righteousness forth as brightness and our salvation as a lamp that burns (Is. 62:1). We need only to say "yes" to Him.

> *WHEN WE ENCOUNTER THIS UNYIELDING LOVE, THIS LOVE SO JEALOUS THAT NO POWER ON THE EARTH CAN PREVAIL AGAINST IT, A FIERCE PEACE EMBRACES OUR TREMBLING HEARTS.*

Bridal Heart

"O my love, you are as beautiful as Tirzah, lovely as Jerusalem, awesome as an army with banners! Turn your eyes away from me, for they have overcome me" (Song Sol. 6:4).

It is not only *His* eyes that are beautifully aflame with love. In this passage in Song of Solomon, the eyes of *the bride* overwhelm the heart of the King. She has just endured the test of love, and Jesus exclaims this glorious statement. Her eyes of faithful devotion and lovesick abandon literally overcome the heart of the mighty God. The Great Conqueror stands conquered by the gaze of the faithful bride. Love Himself is prevailed upon by the love that flows from her heart toward Him.

What does Jesus see in our eyes that has caused Him such delight? He sees the fulfillment of His inheritance promised to Him by His Father for all of time. He perceives a bride flooded with voluntary love, holding a lovesick gaze that pierces through the dim mirror of time and space, reaching the realm of her eternal Desire—Jesus Himself. He is overcome by our eyes of faith as we peer into the mystery of who He is and who we are before Him with only a dim understanding and faint comprehension. It is this act of gazing that causes the Lord to speak one of the strongest statements of scripture about the way His heart is moved by the love of weak human beings. He says, "Turn your eyes away! They overcome Me!"

And at the very center of our being, we are created to exchange this gaze with Him as His eternal spouse. We are created to receive His love and to offer it back to Him wholeheartedly. We were made to enter into this furnace of fiery exchange of desire and affection. The glory of the human spirit is in its God-imparted ability to receive and possess the fiery love of God and to then return it to Him in a flood of contagious desire. His heart is exhilarated with love, and as we open our spirit to Him, He exhilarates us with love as well. He causes us to burn with affections even as He

Himself does. This is our uniqueness among the angels and all of the rest of created order. We were fashioned to love Him with this unyielding single-hearted devotion and to join Him in this communing swirl of affections. It is the most powerful reality of the human spirit.

As we stand in the wake of this torrent of Holy love and desire, from our own hearts will arise supernaturally imparted love for Him. We will cry out "Your love is better than wine, Oh God! (Song Sol. 1:2). Your love is sweeter than the finest things on earth! Your love is the richest of all pleasures and the deepest of all delights." When we walk through the valley of difficulty with darkness veiling our eyes from Him and when our enemy hurls accusations against Him on every side, we will cry out wholeheartedly, "My Beloved is fairer than the sons of men. He is the most gracious of them all! I know what is within His heart. It is an overflowing river of gladness. My Beloved is beautiful and excellent! He is chief among ten thousand! His leadership is perfect! All His ways are just and true!" (Ps.45; Song Sol. 5:10)

THE GLORY OF THE HUMAN SPIRIT IS IN ITS GOD-IMPARTED ABILITY TO RECEIVE AND POSSESS THE FIERY LOVE OF GOD AND TO THEN RETURN IT TO HIM IN A FLOOD OF CONTAGIOUS DESIRE.

The Hidden Glory of Our Lives

"If then you have been raised with Christ, seek those things which are above, where Christ is, sitting at the right hand of God. Set your mind on things above, not on things on earth.

For you died, and your life is hidden with Christ in God.
When Christ who is our life appears, then you also will
appear with Him in glory" (Colossians 3:3-4).

Our glorious destiny and unfathomable future as
the triumphant bride of the Lamb is nearly entirely
hidden from our eyes in this age. God delights in hiding
the treasures of highest worth, and thus He has caused
the full glory and beauty of our lives along with the
wisdom of our decisions for righteousness to be veiled
from us while we live in this natural realm of earth. The
power of our very own lives is virtually concealed from
us. With our natural understandings we have such a
limited grasp of even the smallest fraction of who we
truly are before Him. Yet when we behold Him on that
Day, He will make known to us the truth of our natural
lives on the earth, and we will see the fullness of our
glory. We will stand stunned by the relevance of what
seemed so insignificant on the earth.

Though this very real part of our lives is hidden,
and though in this age we will only ever peer dimly into
it, God desires that we would seek those things that are
above and set our minds on them. "It is the glory of
God to conceal a matter, but
the glory of kings is to search
out a matter" (Prov. 25:2).
Jesus beckons us to come with
Him on a journey of discovering truths about our lives that
the angels can only peer into
with great wonder. He beck-
ons us to come on a process of acquiring understanding
of the truth about our eternal glory. There are magnifi-

HE HAS GIVEN US THE
INVITATION TO LOVE
HIM VOLUNTARILY
WHILE OUR EYES ARE
YET VEILED WITHIN
THE WALLS OF TIME.

cent truths about our lives related to the reality that Jesus is seated at the right hand of God and that we are seated beside Him (Eph. 2:6). He will reveal and unfold these truths to us if we will seek after them. If we search after them as we would search for hidden treasures; He will show them to us in time (Prov. 2:1-5).

As we walk through our days on the earth, we have been given an exceedingly high privilege—an invitation so noble and so grandiose that we will marvel for all eternity at the sheer magnitude of God's wisdom in forming such a gift. He has given us the invitation to love Him voluntarily while our eyes are yet veiled within the walls of time. It is an opportunity to live each day with eyes of faith and revelation set upon that glorious day so real to our future—the marriage supper of the Lamb. He has made a way for us to each day offer up to Him a heart that voluntarily chooses to sow our seeds into the vast unseen, steadfastly certain of their imminent emergence from the soil of eternity. We are given the privilege to choose Him voluntarily with hearts of faith and to live according to the certainty of this hidden mystery of our lives yet to be revealed.

Forever and ever we will live in the reward of these choices. Their value will be revealed and their wisdom vindicated (Matt. 11:19). For thousands upon thousands of years unending, we will dwell in eternity with Him. With unveiled eyes we will behold Him face to face. We will again and again throw our crowns down before Him in the baffling immensity of His splendor. We will be in awe at who we are before Him as we are adorned in all of our beauty. For an everlasting eternity, we will see what was hidden from our eyes while on the earth. Yet it is during this one moment on the earth, this flash of our natural lives, that we have opportunity to love the One in whom we have never seen. "Blessed are those who have not seen and yet have believed" (Jn. 20:29). For one instant, we have the ability to voluntarily choose Him though it seems as utter foolishness to the world. We have been given the chance to lavish our love upon Him though He is nearly entirely hidden from us, and we have been given the opportunity to live as the bride of the Lamb now though we see so dimly. Forever, these choices will ring through the corridors of eternity with resounding worth and relevance.

We live now with that very real day before us, the great wedding day, in continual view! On that day, we will stand together on the sea of glass with all unity, all beauty and all glory. We will declare how exceedingly perfect the Lord's leadership was over our lives and all of human history. Our eyes will behold with brilliant clarity the masterpiece of God's tapestry of time, and we will behold His glorious and excellent leadership in working all things together for the supreme good. We will see how every single aspect of our lives, every individual day and every separate circumstance were arranged to bring forth a prepared bride for the Son of God.

As we behold this majestic orchestration of all of time, the groanings of our earthly lives will be transformed into an awesome thunderous voice of worship. As all of time culminates in this triumphant marriage supper of the Lamb, the greatest event of all history, we will declare with a voice like the sound of many waters and of mighty thunderings, "Alleluia! For the Lord God Omnipotent reigns! Let us be glad and rejoice and give Him glory, for the marriage of the Lamb has come and His wife has made herself ready!"

Truly, Love's pursuit is escorting us to this very actual day in our future. This is where we are going. And before us is the great unfolding. Before us is the journey that will serve as our eternal story of love's exchange never to be forgotten in all the ages to come. We begin this journey with the awakening...

"Wilderness Prayer"

Oh Jesus, my Jesus,
True Friend of my heart, true Lover of my soul,
My heart is hurting. My soul is aching.
All that I have ever been,
All of my "beauties" falling, falling to the ground.
The goodnesses, the righteousness,
The good intentions and "right" motives,
Dropping layer by layer…
Leaving behind one that I do not even know or recognize…
The Lover of my love strips me
And as the hidden things are uncovered
And the exterior beauties taken,
I am not what I thought I was.
I know it is by Your hand that I am stripped.
Though it hurts immensely,
I recognize it as a Love deeper than my heart has ever known
Taking away what will not stand
That He might crown me with His true beauty
And clothe me in His robes.
Truly, I am not the one that I thought myself to be.
They ask me "then who is the one who comes?"
I look only to Your eyes and say,
"She is nothing but what He alone speaks her into being.
His words alone hold within the essence of who she is. She is His.
Do not look upon me, for I am dark.
Please see only Him. He is the beautiful. He is the pure."

CHAPTER 3

AWAKENED TO LOVE

"I charge you, O daughters of Jerusalem, by the gazelles or by the does of the field,
Do not stir up nor awaken love until it pleases" (Song Sol. 2:7).

Before we can give ourselves in whole-hearted pursuit to the worthy Lord, we must be awakened in love. We have sleeping hearts and dull understandings. We do not yet know that our God is truly a God of love and that His love is to be known, experienced and enjoyed by our own hearts. We must be awakened. Our spiritual lives know much barrenness, and only love will remedy our lack of inspiration. For only when we are awakened will we comprehend who He is and the riches He holds in His hand to give our famished hearts.

Yes, the beginning of the journey is in the residence of awakening. Here we are brought from the place of sleep to the place of wakefulness. Though this awakening is first, it does not appear only once in the journey. We are in need of a constant furthering of His reviving of our hearts. We need Him to awaken us over and over again. When He does this, our supposed *contented* hearts are revealed for their true barrenness and escorted to the place of divine dissatisfaction. This is a good thing. It is right where He wants us. Until we are discontent, we will never find ultimate content- ment. Until we are brought out of our spiritual slumber, we will never find the corridor of Love's unfolding. He awakens us that we might begin to hunger for the food of the Bread of Life and thirst for the Living Water.

The awakening of God upon the believer's heart is made manifest by the cry for love that arises from deep within. This is voiced by the maiden in Song of Solomon when she says, "Let Him kiss me with the kisses of His mouth..." (Song Sol. 1:2). We experience an inward cry for more of Jesus. He brings us to a place of deep dissatisfaction in our current spiritual state. As if an interior light goes on, suddenly we become aware of all that we lack and all that we need in God. This may be subtle or even intense. For some it is a gradual desire that grows ever louder with time. For others it is an instant recognition, an abrupt disturbance. We are all at once aware of the present state of our soul, and what was enough yesterday is now utterly inadequate. Which- ever way it manifests, the awakening of God is strategic and transformative to the way we live. We find that we can no longer continue as we have been; we must have more of the Lover of our souls.

> *WE NEED HIM TO AWAKEN US OVER AND OVER AGAIN. WHEN HE DOES THIS, OUR SUPPOSED CONTENTED HEARTS ARE...ESCORTED TO THE PLACE OF DIVINE DISSATISFACTION.*

Though we may not yet know the language, the emerging cry within us is for the kiss of the Word of God upon our hearts. We are longing for an encounter with the Living One, and this encounter happens when God the Word marries with God the Spirit on the inside of our beings, where He dwells. We set ourselves before the Word of God, and when that Word touches the indwelling Spirit within us, a living flame of love is ignited. Spirit meets truth, and true worshippers come forth (Jn. 4:23-24).

When we cry out for this kiss, for this divine enflaming, we desire what we were in fact created for: intimacy with Jesus Christ. We desire to be true worshipers just as the Father is seeking, those who enter the worship that arises from the spiritual kiss of the Word and the Spirit within our very beings. We cry, "O Father! Let Your Son, the Living Word, kiss this weak heart of mine and awaken me in love!" We recognize our need and cry out for its fulfillment. We ask for the One, who awakens love and causes it to abound, to now come and cause such abundance in this heart. We ask the living Word to join with the Holy Spirit in our inner man, and there become a burning fire within.

God the Awakener

"I awakened You under the apple tree..." (Song Sol. 8:5).

When we cry out for His awakening, we are responding to the divine invitation He has already issued our own hearts. When He causes our hearts to cry out for encounter, it is actually His own invitation to us at work within our souls. We are not bidding God to come

39

to us, as if we had just thought of the idea. Rather, we are entering into and participating in the *ever-standing* calling of God over our lives. He summons us into our eternal inheritance in knowing Him.

When we call on Him to awaken our hearts in love, we are taking our place of agreement with His own invitation. We do this by positioning our hearts before His love and asking Him to accomplish in us what He has already determined before the foundations of the world.

It takes God to love God. It takes the power of God on the human heart for the human heart to move in love for God. He is the One who awakens love in our hearts. To seek to describe the journey of the human heart, we must begin with Him, for He is forever the Beginning and the End. It never begins with us; He causes love to awaken. He is the King who brings us into the chambers of Divine love (Song Sol. 1:4). He has brought, is bringing and will continue to bring each of us into His chambers, the places where we experience His love. When we recognize love, hunger and desire within our hearts, we can be sure that God has already touched us by awakening us. When this cry for greater love arises from within, we can know that a holy invitation has already been at work in our souls and that He has already brought us into the chambers of love's exchange.

> *WHEN HE CAUSES OUR HEARTS TO CRY OUT FOR ENCOUNTER, IT IS ACTUALLY HIS OWN INVITATION TO US AT WORK WITHIN OUR SOULS.*

He alone knows the timing and the method in which to awaken us. We see His strategic awakening several times throughout our journey as depicted in the Song of Solomon. Three times throughout the Song, He exhorts the daughters to not awaken the heart of His bride until love so desires (2:7; 3:5; 8:4). As we cooperate with Him, the Holy Spirit awakens love within us in stages. He is continually in a process of bringing forth deeper love within us, causing us to become awakened at key times along our way. In the beginning, He awakens us to the journey of love; we are stirred to know Him in deeper intimacy. Along the way, He reveals to us many different faces of Jesus, this God-Man to whom we have joined ourselves.

Because of the pain that hunger and desire for Him cause us, we often disregard the power of this gift of God's awakening. We are only aware that we want Him to come in greater ways and that, as far as we can tell, He is not coming. We forget that He was and is the Initiator of this entire process, and we fail to recognize that He has indeed already entrusted our souls with something great. He has given us a true gift in this insistent cry within us for more of Him. The Awakener, Jesus, has given us the gift of an awakened heart.

Awakened to the Highest Pleasure

"...For Your love is better than wine" (Song Sol. 1:2).

The love of Jesus is the highest pleasure of the human heart. If we were to search heaven and earth, we would find this to be true. In all of the wonderful pleasures of life, in this age and the age to come, the supreme enjoyment of life is in the exchange of love with the Person of Jesus Christ. There is no greater reward. His love is the highest, the richest, the most pleasing of all.

In this first passage of the Song of Solomon, the bride asks for the kiss of God's word because she knows the inevitable result of experiencing it: her heart will be satisfied in the superior pleasure of God alone. She exclaims, "Let Him kiss me…for Your love is better than wine." The high pleasure of the wine of His love is set up to contrast all lesser pleasures. His love is better than wine, better than all secondary pleasures. His love and the experience of the exchange of love between our hearts and His own is the highest of our earthly reward. When we enter into the experience of this superior pleasure, our drive for the lesser pleasures is overcome.

This cry for the kiss of God is more than the acknowledgment of our own need and desire. It is the actual *sight* and *vision* of what is offered by Jesus to anyone who will receive. We are not only awakened to our own need; our eyes are opened to the high vision of what the Lord would freely give to us if we would but search and find it in Him. We not only see the vacant barrenness in our own hearts, we perceive the unsearchable plentitude He holds and desires to give to us— "'Eye has not seen, nor ear heard, nor have entered into the heart of man the things which God has prepared for those who love Him'" (1 Cor. 2:9). We begin to see our inheritance in God. He cracks open the door to see what is behind the knocking, and He gives but a peek into what the one who seeks shall find. When He captivates us by this vision of our inheritance in Him, it is nothing short of a divine invitation. He is beckoning, alluring us, drawing us to come after Him and take hold of what He so desires to give us.

Responding to the Awakening of God

"Listen, O daughter, consider and incline your ear; forget your own people also and your father's house; so the King will greatly desire your beauty..." (Ps. 45:10-11).

God refuses to open up the mysteries of His heart to the unwanting soul. He wants us to search for Him as for hidden treasure, leaving no stone unturned. He beckons us as a daughter to consider and incline our ear to Him...to turn our hearts toward Him as our Husband, leaving our father's house and joining ourselves to Him. The way that He allures and motivates us to this kind of wholehearted pursuit is through the revelation of His enjoyment over us.

The King greatly desires my beauty. This is the motivational method in which we move toward Him in love. His invitation and awakening causes desire in our hearts to arise in holy pursuit. We become zealous over our own hearts—that all the hindrances would be removed so that we may encounter Love in fullness. In this search, we respond to His invitation to leave all our former ways behind.

> *WE BEGIN TO SEE OUR INHERITANCE IN GOD. HE CRACKS OPEN THE DOOR TO SEE WHAT IS BEHIND THE KNOCKING, AND HE GIVES BUT A PEEK INTO WHAT THE ONE WHO SEEKS SHALL FIND.*

We leave our father's house because we are compelled by love. The father's house represents all the natural definitions, positive or negative, by which we once defined our lives. It is time that we determine our significance by one Voice alone. And it is the voice of the Bridegroom that so fuels our flight. We have heard a sweeter song.

An awakened heart cannot remain in one place, as though uninformed. It must give up everything to find the One Desire of its affections. We venture out into the wilderness as one betrothed in search for our Beloved even as Rebekah left everything and set out on a journey in search of Isaac (Gen. 24). We know not what lies ahead, but we have been awakened to the love of this Man Jesus, and His desire for us has stirred us into pursuit. With expectant hearts, we give ourselves to the journey before us, knowing that the end is marriage, and that marriage unimaginable.

He has set up His kingdom in such a way that a partnering is required in the receiving. The riches of His heart are there to be discovered, but only by those who would search and find them—"And you will seek Me and find Me, when you search for Me with all your heart. I will be found by you, says the LORD..." (Jer. 29:13-14). Divine romance forbids it to be otherwise. If He were to reveal all things to all men without any search or any pursuit, it would be a one-sided exchange. We would experience all the benefits of His love and never find the delight of searching and finding, of knocking and being opened to. He would be doing us a severe disfavor to not hide His treasure from us. He knew that He would not be found by the casual glancers but, oh, the persistent gazers! How they will find Him! He has kept the treasury of the knowledge of God for the lovers. Only the hungry and desirous will find Him.

Solomon gives the process of encounter in Proverbs two. He says,

> "My son, if you receive my words, and treasure my commands within you, so that you incline your ear to wisdom, and apply your heart to understanding; yes, if you cry out for discernment, and lift up your voice for understanding, if you seek her as silver, and search for her as for hidden treasures; then you will understand the fear of the Lord, and find the knowledge of God" (Prov. 2:1-5).

The knowledge of God, the knowing of His heart, is acquired through a steadfast searching. It is a pursuit so relentless and persevering that it is compared to the search of hidden treasure.

God gives Himself to those who seek for Him. What empowers the seeking is the revelation that He is indeed treasure. He reveals His heart to those who pursue Him.

GOD GIVES HIMSELF TO THOSE WHO SEEK FOR HIM. WHAT EMPOWERS THE SEEKING IS THE REVELATION THAT HE IS INDEED TREASURE.

And those who pursue Him are those who love Him because they see value where others do not. Lovers always find what the others give up searching for. Surely those who give their lives in affectionate pursuit of Him will find the treasure of their search, the knowledge of God.

Awakened in the Wilderness

"'...But the friend of the Bridegroom, who stands and hears Him, rejoices greatly because of the Bridegroom's voice. Therefore this joy of mine is fulfilled'" (Jn. 3:29).

The Lord leads the awakened heart straight into the wilderness. Yet before we rush into false conclusions, let us remember that He is not angry in this leading. We have false ideas about Him and about His purposes in the "wilderness." He does not bring us out into the desert to discipline us in His deep displeasure.

SURELY THOSE WHO GIVE THEIR LIVES IN AFFECTIONATE PURSUIT OF HIM WILL FIND THE TREASURE OF THEIR SEARCH, THE KNOWLEDGE OF GOD.

Rather, He is a God with tender love in His eyes, desiring that we might know His love in fullness and not in part. He brings us into this desert region even as He brought the one who was the forerunner of Jesus, so that we might hear the voice of the Bridegroom there and find the fulfillment of our joy. In His jealousy over us, He desires to draw us away for a season that He might win us fully to Himself. It is out of this movement of love in His heart that He allures us into the wilderness (Hos. 2:14).

The wilderness is the meeting point between the God of love and the barren soul. Outwardly, we come away for a time, leaving much of the noise and clutter of our many activities and all that is constantly grabbing for our attentions. We get alone with our God in the quiet place of the heart and seek to hear the Bridegroom's voice that He might make us fully His own. The wilderness is the place where all of our secondary loves are revealed and where we are stripped of false affections and other masters besides Him. He leads us into this place of encounter so that His voice, the voice of the Bridegroom, might be heard from among all the other lesser voices. Here Jesus becomes the only Love and only Lord of our lives.

Oh, how necessary is this initial quieting of all the extra voices and noises that surround the soul. For only in their quieting is our inward noise revealed. When we pull away from the whirlwind of activity, instead of peace on the inside, we find yet a greater storm in need of God's quieting. We thought that all we needed was outward peace, but when all is outwardly quiet, the inner turbulence continues at a steady rapidity. Our souls do not know how to be before God in the stillness of intimacy. We have allowed many voices and many opinions of man to dominate our lives, leaving us with a great deal of inward disorder.

When we seek to encounter God in this solitary season, instead of finding rest and peace, we are at first disoriented and in pain. The reason for this disorientation is that we have derived our identity and our comfort from a thousand false places, and when we are without those false comforts and alone with the one true Comfort, we do not know how to receive His affections. We are not at rest in His presence because we are yet so unlike Him. Instead of finding peace before His eyes (Song Sol. 8:10) we squirm beneath His gaze.

In this wilderness, we not only discover the presence of so much internal clutter, but we see the absence of our spiritual reality. We discover our own internal wilderness. We are spiritually barren. The reality in God that we thought we possessed we do not possess at all. Our language cannot help us here. The opinions of man do us no favors. We are before one gaze and His is the only one that counts. We realize how little we know of Him and how many things we have clung to other than Him. Yet this is the perfect place for our souls to be in. For it is in the discovering of our barrenness and in the quieting of our clamoring inner lives that we will find the sweetness of the Bridegroom God's voice. It is for this purpose that He brought us here.

We cannot lose heart when these initial tensions begin to arise. We must know even at the beginning that we will encounter pain in our own soul in this time. There is a definite struggle and a certain affliction to this wilderness as we seek to draw near to Him and are confronted with all the clutter and noises in our inner lives. There is a sure delay in the process of these noisy voices succumbing under the lordship of the Voice like many waters. Yet we must not grow faint with discouragement in the delay. We must remain in the stretchings of this conflict of soul and continue to wait for the breaking in of His voice of affection. We must find comfort in the fact that it is for this reason He has brought us to this wilderness: to find the Bridegroom's voice. Surely, He will come and bring comfort to our waiting hearts as we are transformed into His likeness.

In order to come to a place of peace before His eyes, exchanging the identity we have received from man for the true and living identity that only God defines, a certain death must transpire. In this wilderness of the soul, God sovereignly arranges opportunity for our death and His life to interface. He invites us to leave all of our old definitions and all our soulish clingings. He asks us even to embrace a place of dangling as we wait for the Bridegroom's voice to bring true definition to our waiting hearts. It is here in this place, away from onlookers and alone with God, that we die and begin to truly live. We learn to leave false strengths and to embrace utter weakness in all humility. For only in weakness is His strength perfected and made full.

It is time that our souls come into alignment with the truth of God for there alone will we find rest. We learn to leave our false comforts so that He alone might be the consolation of our souls. Only He can teach us how to define ourselves not by falsehoods but by the truth of His love. This does not happen automatically but day by day in this wilderness as we learn to rewrite the untruths within us through continual agreement with the truth of who God is.

He has us right where He desires us. We are in the trenches of transformation. And this transformation comes through nothing less than love in its richness reforming our hearts. Though we encounter times of great difficulty and pain in these trenches, there is no substitute for the Love that we discover. He has not tricked us to bring us here; for though we feel its quietness, the wilderness truly is the place of encounter. Though we experience the pain of the absence of many old comforts and the presence of our great barrenness; Jesus is not absent in this place. In this vulnerable state, He causes Love to utterly conquer us. When we would expect the most disappointment and discipline, He gives unending kindness and mercy. He overcomes us with His love. The Lord has brought us to this place that He might become our one Comfort, answering our desires with Himself. He brings us into this desert in order to reveal His unrelenting love to us and fill our barrenness with the fullness of Himself.

Where a heart has discovered its utter barrenness, God may reveal His plentitude. He encounters us in this place of emptiness. As we are alone with Him and all the other voices are quieted, the Lord begins to engage our hearts with His love. He begins to comfort our souls with His great desire and matchless tenderness. He whispers, "Do you know how much I love you? Do you know My desire?" He draws our hearts by both the high vision of His purpose for us and by His affectionate desire. At His marvelous generosity, we become willing to do whatever it takes to know and enter into the vast riches of our inheritance in Him.

> *WHERE A HEART HAS DISCOVERED ITS UTTER BARRENNESS, GOD MAY REVEAL HIS PLENTITUDE.*

Now that we have responded to His awakening and followed Him into the wilderness of encounter, we are prepared to receive His love in the greatest measure. We are "alone with the Alone" and in the perfect place to undergo the transformation of His love. Our hearts are positioned to come face to face with Love Himself and to personally receive from Him ...

Gaze Eternal

Oh Gaze Eternal,
How penetrating are Your Fires
Rushing through my darkest places
With the burning streams of Desire
Leaving me naked, purged and bare
...Yet embraced

Refusing all my offers
To earn Your love,
To win Your gaze,
To deserve Your smile,
You wrap Your heavy love around me,
Until my anxious arguments subside.

You take hold of my weakest places
And kiss them with Your mercy
Lifting up my low grounds,
With Your mighty love so holy.

Burning Affections, consuming me,
And transforming my darkness with light
Jealous Ardor refusing to be denied
Yet engulfing all that hides...in me

Oh Gaze Eternal,
How penetrating are Your fires
Oh Friend Eternal,
How you win my heart
With unprecedented, unmerited Desire

CHAPTER 4

FACE TO FACE WITH LOVE

"Let Him kiss me with the kisses of His mouth—for Your love is better than wine" (Song Sol. 1:2).

Sitting in a movie theater by myself one afternoon, watching a modern day version of the fairy tale *Cinderella*, the Lord assailed the inner chambers of my heart with a divine arrow. I went to this *Cinderella* story with expectation. I desired that the Lord speak to me and make sense in my heart of the classic story of all time. My heart was in a season of wrestling with the possibility of a lovesick God. How could the magnificent, brilliant God who is perfect and holy and glorious fall in love with weak human beings who are fallen and broken and sinful?

In a scene toward the end of the movie, the Lord answered the brewing questions of my heart. The girl playing Cinderella was being held captive when the prince arrived to rescue her. He rode in as a strong hero, dressed in all of his dashing and royal attire, and in a climatic moment, his eyes met hers. The tension of his royalty and her "commonness" rose to a climax as she realized he saw her as she was, only a peasant. In every past encounter, she managed just in time to be dressed and adorned beautifully, as a noble woman. Yet,

THERE IS LITTLE ROOM FOR HUMAN REASONING WHEN THE GOD WHOSE LOVE THAT SURPASSES KNOWLEDGE HAS SET HIS AFFECTION UPON US.

in that moment, she was dressed in rags, dirty from head to toe, with nowhere to escape. She bowed her head in shame as he approached. The prince dismounted from his horse, knelt in front of her, and with lovesick eyes, seeing only beauty and the one desired, he said, *"I kneel before you not as a prince, but as a man in love, but I would feel like a king if you would be my wife."*

These are the words that broke open a deep place within me. The truth of God came in like a flood against my false ideas about God and realigned the crooked places, making them straight. The flood of truth was simply this: *"He is a Man in love!"* I realized that I had lost sight of the *irrational, lovesick* part of love and that I had been trying to reason my way through an illogical reality. Where is logic found in lovesickness? When a man is in love, what can his beloved do with him? She can present her arguments and try to persuade him otherwise. She can tell him how undeserving she is and how unreasonable is his affection. Yet with every argument, he will look at her with an incoherent lovesick gaze, unwavered by her line of reasoning. Truly there is little hope for common sense if lovesickness has prevailed upon a heart. And there is little room for human reasoning when the God whose love that surpasses knowledge has set His affection upon us.

When the Lord opened up my understanding to receive this new revelation of the nature of His love, He rearranged something deep within me. With many tears that night I wrote these words:

"Love Me"

But why? But how? How is it that He loves me?
How is it that the King, the Creator, the Beautiful and the Mighty
Has vowed to love and adore me? How can it be so?
And I so dirty… I so unlovely…I so dark.
And Him so pure…Him so Fair…Him so good…How is it so?
Jesus, I do not understand. Jesus, what have You done?
It is too much. It is too great a thing…for one so undeserving.
Yet even in this You delight. You love me in my weakness.
You love me in my helplessness.
You do not ask me to be strong.
You do not ask me to first be deserving.
For I shall never deserve such a love.
It is based not on my deserving. It is based not on my earnings.
All that I could ever do would never be enough.
It would never cause my heart to be found worthy.
And you delight in it to be this way.
You cause my attempts to be found empty and my strivings to end dry.
For never will You love me for them.
Your love for me is too rich and too great to be bought at so low a price.
It is a love I could never afford, nor am asked to pay a penny for.
It is mine. Freely it is mine. Given as a free gift.
What all the kings and princes of the world could not afford,
You have handed to my little heart.
What love is this, my Jesus, and why do You love me?
Oh, why have You cast Your riches and Your wealth

to such a soul as mine?
If I had the strength I would say,
"Please…for justice's sake…love another."
But I cannot say such words. A fool I would be to turn You away.
Love me then, oh Perfect King. Love the poor and dirty.
Love the one who cannot earn nor pay. Love the despised and rejected.
Love one who can bring You nothing except the tears of a lovesick heart.
Love me. For I cannot turn You away. I cannot deny such love
Love me then, my Jesus. As You have vowed, love and adore little me…

The Truth of His Love

Jesus, the sovereign King and reigning Lord, is a Bridegroom, and He has set His affections on weak human beings. It is the most remarkable story of the ages, and our natural logic cannot make sense of it. Our response to this *Cinderella* scene is an ever so faint representation of our flawed understanding of the story of the ages. We rationalize that the powerful prince cannot desire the unattractive peasant girl; it just isn't right. Yet this is the logic that reasons us right out of enjoying the glory of our inheritance and eternal destiny.

It is a Love surpassing knowledge that He has bestowed upon us. Our natural minds cannot and will not make sense of it. So long as we remain in the position of human reasoning, we can reel ourselves round and round the issue, and we will never receive the truth of His love. It is as inconceivable and unimaginable as the fairy tales, and it is even exceedingly beyond them. Yet it is the truth, and truth is not determined by our logic. Truth is defined by the One who *is* Truth. And the One who has set His zealous affections on weak human beings is *the Way, the Truth and the Life* (Jn. 14:6). What is true is what is found within His heart.

The fairy tales were written out of our God-given desire and hope that such a story might actually be true of our lives. It *is* our story. With fervent zeal, He has arranged all of time to unfold as the most remarkable fairy tale of the ages and to culminate in the greatest wedding of all of history. And the wedding is only the beginning! For eternity we will live in His embrace as His cherished bride as He forever stuns us with His beauty and glory. Our living testimony is that the glorious God has allowed His heart to be overcome by weak human beings, and He has given Himself to both the exhilarations and the woundings of a lovesick heart. When He gazes upon me, He sees through the eyes of love and desire. He comes before me and says, "I am a Man in love. I am a God that burns with desire, and I have set My affections on you. I am an all consuming fire of love, and you are the inheritance that My Father has promised me. Will you receive My love?"

Receiving His Love

The first part of encountering His love is the revelation of His desire for me and who He is as the Lover of my soul. The second part is actually *receiving* that love and beginning to drink deeply of its treasury. Our role as the bride of the Lamb is to open our hearts wide and *receive*. And this is a progressive journey for we can only receive as much as our hearts are enlarged to take in. His Being is an endless ocean, and who can contain Him? Who can fathom His eternal personality? We have small hearts, and our capacities are shrunk by the drought of this age and the unrenewed desert of our understandings. How is it that this vast ocean of love can be taken in by a small human heart? The only way that our hearts are expanded to receive is by the supernatural broadening of our capacities through the divine stretchings of hunger, longing and desire. These inner forces carve out space within us and make room for love.

THE ONLY WAY THAT OUR HEARTS ARE EXPANDED TO RECEIVE IS BY THE SUPERNATURAL BROADENING OF OUR CAPACITIES THROUGH THE DIVINE STRETCHINGS OF HUNGER, LONGING AND DESIRE.

We come before His fiery affections day after day and open our hearts to Him. We posture ourselves to receive the River of Pleasures that flows freely from His heart. As we do this, He awakens longing in us through the revelation of His love and then gives Himself to us based on our hunger and desire—"'Blessed are those who mourn, for they shall be comforted…. Blessed are those who hunger and thirst for righteousness, for they shall be filled'" (Matt. 5:4, 6). As we wait on Him, He reveals Himself to us and our hearts grow in longing and desire. These cravings then prepare the place to receive more of His love and greater understanding of all that is in His heart.

And what does it mean to come before the Fire of Desire? We fill our minds with the scriptures that speak of His affections, and we meditate on who He is in His personality. We sing and speak the written Word over our hearts again and again like a gentle rain watering a dry and arid land. We cannot afford to take this flippantly. We set our gaze on this glad-hearted Jesus and behold Him in His beauty by peering into the windows God has revealed to us in the Word. We allow our old paradigms to be transformed by the Holy Spirit as we gaze on Him in the new light of His immeasurable love. It's a slow transformation with many delays. It doesn't happen in a day's or a week's time. Yet as the weeks turn to months and the months multiply into years, we will look back and see an undeniable transformation. Our view of Him and of ourselves will undergo immense conversion. Whether we initially perceive it or not, we will reap the Spirit. We will behold Him rightly and view ourselves in the truth of who we are.

To be His bride is to respond to His gaze of affection as one with all dignity and honor, for a bride knows who she is and does not question her position before His eyes. She knows that she stands before a God who is overcome with love. She is not afraid when the enemy comes and brings accusations and lies. When in the wake of troublesome circumstances, she does not fear or question the love of her Beloved. Instead she stands fearless in love, with all dignity and honor and says, *"He loves me. I know that He loves me. His leadership is perfect and all His ways are love."* This will be our testimony. We will be as a bride in all of her glory—a bride that does not fear. We will be a bride that stands and believes in the love of her Bridegroom God and ascends far above the cares of this world in the divine chariot of His eternal affections.

Transformed by the Knowledge of His Love

Our God is the All Consuming Fire. His fiery love is not neutral in its effects upon our hearts. When we come into this Fire, we do not remain the same. His jealous love burns away all the things within us that are not everlasting and purifies all that will remain forever. There are places in each of our minds that stand in opposition to the truths of His love and His character. These areas of accusation stand against the true knowledge of His heart. When we purposefully labor to daily set our hearts before this God of raging desire, He burns away the false understandings and imparts living knowledge of Himself.

HIS FIERY LOVE IS NOT NEUTRAL IN ITS EFFECTS UPON OUR HEARTS.

As we behold Him, our eyes become filled with light. As we gaze upon Him and the truth of His personality enters our hearts, we are transformed. In His light we see light. We begin to perceive our life on the earth and our destiny in eternity so differently than we used to. As we enter into the revelation of His love, our hearts become realigned. There are things within us that are out of line with the truth of God's heart and must be made straight. There are accusations of the enemy that we have unknowingly agreed with. These are set straight by the love of God.

Repetition of His Love

We have weak hearts and feeble memories. What He told us yesterday about His pleasure in us seems so distant today. We so easily drift from truth and lose touch with the intimacy we have known only yesterday. Though we might have been set ablaze with the knowledge of God's abounding love and the certainty of His affection then, today, it seems more like a fantasy as the grey of this life hovers over us and refuses to give way to the light of His love. Though it felt like a steady river then, today, it is a dry bed. *"Tell me again,"* we whisper. *"Tell me again. I'm not sure how I forgot, but tell me again. What was it about Your desire? How is it again that You feel for me? I need to know it all anew today. Jesus, tell me again."*

As we learn to receive His love into the chambers of our hearts, we will find a constant need for repetition and reiteration of His affections. It is part of the process of love to continuously request, *"Tell me again about Your love for me. Tell me how You delight in me. Remind me of Your affections."* We will find ourselves in a tug of war between experiencing His enjoyment and absolutely losing touch of it. In these times when His love seems so faint in our memories, we must continually sing what He has spoken in His Word about His love for us over our hearts. We must ask His Spirit to once more remind us. Jesus knew that our hearts would need this and gave us the Holy Spirit to bring to our remembrance all that He has spoken to us (Jn. 14:26). He knew that we would need the continual reassurance that all was true and that our hope was not in vain. Therefore, we must persistently ask the Holy Spirit to reignite our hearts with the truths of His love for us, crying out, *"Tell me again!"*

> IT IS PART OF THE PROCESS OF LOVE TO CONTINUOUSLY REQUEST, *"TELL ME AGAIN ABOUT YOUR LOVE FOR ME…"*

A Voluntary Love

In the ancient Jewish wedding betrothal ceremony, after the groom presented the marriage contract to the parents of the bride and the bride herself, he turned for the singular acceptance of the bride. To see if his beloved received his proposal, the young man would pour a cup of wine for her, drink from it himself and then wait to see if she drank it. This cup was a symbol of covenant relationship. In drinking of the cup, she said, "Yes," to his proposal, the covenant was sealed, and they were betrothed. In the same way, Jesus our eternal Bridegroom performed the legal contract of redemption, and He now places the cup of covenant in front of each of us individually and asks, "Will you have ALL of Me?

The kind of love He covets is the kind that arises *willingly* from each individual. He desires a voluntary "yes" to come forth from our hearts. What lies in our future is not an arranged marriage without choice; we will volunteer our love freely. For what is love when it is not chosen? In His perfect sovereignty and violent desire, He created the human heart with the free will. He desired voluntary lovers. "Your people shall be volunteers in the day of Your power..." (Ps. 110:3) He leaves room for the voice of our choice. As sovereign Leader, He does not use His authority to mandate or dictate love for Himself. Rather, in His thunderous power He commands the way to be made for the sound of each small voice to arise in the form of agreement with His love. He wants hearts that choose Him even as a bride chooses her husband and says yes to his proposal. This clear *yes* must resound from our hearts in order to plunge into the depths of His love.

As He places the cup in front of us, He asks, "Will you receive all that I am?" It is no small question that He asks of us. To receive all of Him is an unfathomable venture. It is a *yes* not contingent on His fitting into our understanding or having a full comprehension of Him and His ways. We join ourselves to all that He is without understanding in our minds even a tiny portion of who He is. And it is a dangerous consent that we give Him. By all earthly means, it is no safer than joining ourselves to an ocean or cleaving to a whirlwind. It is no more secure to our natural understandings than becoming one with fire. Even so, it is, in truth, the safest and most pleasurable of all unions. It is a fierce decision of love we make because of our fierce propensity to want to know exactly what He might do and where He might take us. Yet with all of our unfamiliarity with His ways, this "yes" to *all that He is* is our wise choice on the earth.

Though we see dimly and we cannot know all that we are agreeing to, we agree to Love, always Love. We know the heart of this Ocean is always love. What safer realm is there than this? Our natural minds have not fathomed the deep refuge and peace that abides there. It is the peace that passes understanding and the love that surpasses knowledge. Oh, how safe is the dwelling place of God! Oh, how secure is the bride of His choice in the treasured place of His embrace! And oh, the pleasure in that embrace!!

Ours is a God whose personality is so vast and inexhaustible that we will spend all of eternity never reaching the end of its unfoldings. And He has created our hearts with a divine desire to give ourselves to this endless search. Yes, we are joined to an Ocean of boundless mystery. We tremble before His greatness while endlessly desiring more of the unveiling of our Beloved Husband. Forever and ever we will remain fascinated, in holy awe at His beauty and greatness. How brilliant and radiant is the All Consuming Fire! How awesome is this Violent Whirlwind! How wonderful is this Ocean we have thrown our hearts into!

"Joined to an Ocean"

I join myself to an Ocean.
I give myself to an All Consuming Fire.
Who can know what I have said yes to?
Or where this yes will take me?
Worlds of vastness abide within You.
Uncharted waters. Deep unknown.
Yes. I say, "Yes." To all that You are.
It isn't the kind of choice in which I know all that I say yes to,
Only in part do I know and only that dimly.
How could I possibly know all that is in Your heart?
How could I fathom what has burned within You from everlasting?
I could never comprehend where that fire has been or where it is going.
I could never fathom what lies within the deep of that Ocean.
I join myself to an Everlasting Fire of Desire,
And I make my bed within Eternal Deep.
When I look into the fiery gaze of the Everlasting Bridegroom,
How could I know the history and the story behind that fire?
For it has burned since before time began.
Generation after generation, it has cultivated its fiery story,
And who could know its tale?

I say, "Yes," to all that You are. To all that is in your heart.
Unknown mystery. Unknown Ocean.
Unutterable Wisdom and Transcendent heights of Glory.
I throw myself into the unknown vastness of Thy Person.
How great is the deep of all that I have not fathomed about You.
Where this will take me I have no knowing.
Yet I know that love will ever be the banner over me.
For Your works are just and true and all Your ways are Love.
This is what I do know of You
And what will be my testimony until the end.
I join myself to an Ocean. I give myself to a Divine world unknown.
And I will follow the Lamb.
I will follow that Man wherever He goes.

"My Song"

He wrote a song long ago
Inscribed on my heart for me.
A song comprised for my heart to sing
For all eternity.
Deep in my heart, waters deep
Composition sweet.
Hidden for His heart alone
The Divine hidden within me.
Words unexpressed by another's heart
Unfounded in all the earth.
Only deep within this soul
The satisfaction of His search
For the place in His heart
It was fashioned to touch.
He awakens the sleeping love.
He draws forth the deep waters,
And by my voice
He is overcome

CHAPTER 5

PERSONAL RECEIVING

"My dove, my perfect one, is the only one, the only one of her mother, the favorite of the one who bore her" (Song Sol. 6:9).

What do you do when the Man with fire in His eyes narrows His gaze and looks entirely and only upon you? What happens when this Bridegroom King singles you out in the large crowd of the human race and begins to invade you with His affections? What responses come forth from your heart?

When Jesus our Savior becomes Jesus our Bridegroom in our understanding and He begins to reveal His deep affection for us personally, suddenly we find ourselves in a whirlwind of new tensions. All kinds of new things, both good and bad, begin to rise from our hearts. We find that though we were comfortable with Him proclaiming His love to the entire crowd, we become terrified to be alone in the ocean of His love. We begin to resist and uncomfortably squirm beneath the weight of His desire.

The God that "so loved the world" remains only
a *nice* God until that "world" becomes *you*. If it contin-
ues to be only "corporate" in our understandings, and
we merely receive the truth that He so loved "the
world," it will not ever change the inner parts of our
hearts. If we accept this revelation of Jesus as our
Bridegroom only in the corporate sense without labor-
ing for a personal comprehension of it, then we become
like the foolish virgins who knew that He was a Bridegroom but lost the light of their lamps in the critical
hour because they had not cultivated intimacy with Him
personally.

What makes a bride a bride is that she knows
that she stands utterly alone in the eyes of her beloved.
She knows that she is the unique one and the favorite
of her husband. This is why it is so crucial that each
heart goes on a *personal* journey of bridal love. We each
have to stand alone within the fire of His gaze and
allow His affections to be deeply personal. We have to
know and feel like the favorite of the Lord, standing
utterly alone in His narrow gaze of desire.

Most of us can receive the *idea* that God is in
love. We accept the *concept* that He burns with desire.
Yet we do not plunge our own hearts into the revolu-
tionary truth that He is ravished over *me personally*. This
personal part touches places within us that the corporate part does not. It reaches into us as an invasion and
interfaces with the deepest core of who we are. We
begin to ask ourselves questions like, "How could He
desire me above all the others and yet love all the others
in the same way He loves me? How is it that He is

jealous for me personally when I stand as one of many amidst the entire corporate Bride of Christ?"

When I found myself in my own journey under the flood of these questions, He revealed to me a small picture of how this individual love takes place in His heart. He revealed to me how it is possible that each one of us could be His favorite and stand in that unique position of privilege before His eyes. He showed me that within His great musical heart were many songs. He created one person to sing a unique song of His heart. The Creator placed within the deep places of every created heart a specific song from His own being. He brought forth each person in His image as a song to delight His heart. Only that person, with that frame, history and journey could answer and fulfill His desire for his or her specific place in His heart.

> NO ONE EXCEPT ME COULD FULFILL THE PURPOSE OF MY LIFE AND SING THE SONG THAT ANSWERS MY SPECIFIC PLACE IN THE HEART OF GOD.

When I understood that I was a song that originated in the heart of God before there was time and I was created from and for a very specific desire in His heart, I began to deeply receive His personal affections for me. No one except me could fulfill the purpose of my life and sing the song that answers my specific place in the heart of God. He awaits my response alone. When I began to feel this uniqueness, totally new emotions began to spring forth from my heart. When I touched the emotions of being *His favorite*, the realm of His affections opened up a whole new world of enjoyment. I began to feel urgency to respond and to answer

Him with what He desired: my agreement with His love. He desires that I say, "Yes," to His very personal love for me and take my position of privilege in His heart.

You in Me

"At that day you will know that I am in My Father, and YOU IN ME, and I in you" (Jn. 14:20, emphasis added).

"You are in Me," He said. We have heard the words "I am in My Father" and even that "I am in you" but have we heard Him say to our hearts, *"You are in Me?"* He points to each heart individually and says, *"You are within Me."* I am within His heart. I dwell there. It is where I came from, where I reside and where I will return. I abide there in Him just as He abides within me. I am seated with Him in heavenly places. My life is hidden with Christ in God. When He appears, then I also will appear with Him in glory (Col. 3:4). It is not only that His Spirit, the indwelling Christ, lives within me. It is that I, the cherished bride of His choosing, dwell within His heart—a mutual residency, a holy communion.

He created me out of part of Himself. Within me He fashioned a reflection of His glory, a portion of His great mystery, a living, breathing image of Himself. It is as though He reached into His great Personhood and drew out a living substance to breathe into my feeble body. Every part of who I am lends itself to the enhancement of that divine treasure within. He aligned my frame, personality, mind, weakness and strength to reflect this beautiful portion of Himself. He placed me on the earth on the day of my birth and said, "Now that portion of my heart may live in time and space. Now that mystery of My personality may have reflection and image."

The way that I enter this great mystery is through agreement—my agreement with *who He is* and then *who I am* flowing out of that. The Holy Spirit, whom He breathed into me at the newbirth, daily ushers me into the true understanding of who God is. He reveals Jesus to my heart, and as I behold His beauty, I am transformed from glory to glory. Proceeding from this revelation of who He is is the revelation of who I am *in Him.* When He created me He said to the Father, "This is good." He agreed with His work in my creation. I must also come into deep agreement with Him, joining Him in His pleasure. As I agree with what He has created within me, I come into union with Him, no longer separated by any hindrance or falsity. I agree with Christ within me without any argument or disagreement. In this, I become who I truly am—who He created me to be. Jesus is formed within me, and the glorious divine treasure that He has placed within me begins to shine forth in brilliance.

Throughout the entire journey of life in this age, we are coming into that which we have been in His heart for all eternity and living in the full measure of that reality. He created each one in His likeness that, in every life, He might be further revealed. He arranges our pasts and governs our present and future circumstances in order to bring us into this fullness. Thus, should we not have great zeal to partner with Him in removing every obstacle and throwing off all hindrances so we might enter into all that He has ordained for our own hearts? We have but a moment on the earth to believe in this mystery and reach for it. Then forever with Him, we will live in the fullness of our greatness before Him. Oh, that the Creator Himself might shine forth in the divine beauty of the Godhead that He placed uniquely within each heart!

Each heart is a window into the Beloved Jesus Himself, and we together are the fullness, a suitable companion to the Man Christ Jesus. This is the key to loving one another. If every heart gives revelation into what our Beloved is like and each individual possesses a great secret about His personality, will we not love one another with great fervency and fascination? We will begin to love each other not out of duty but out of holy expectation for greater revelation of the heart of our Lord. "…That you… may be able to comprehend *with all the saints* what is the width and length and depth and height—to know the love of Christ which passes knowledge; that you may be filled with all the fullness of God" (Eph. 3:17-19).

> *OH, THAT THE CREATOR HIMSELF MIGHT SHINE FORTH IN THE DIVINE BEAUTY OF THE GODHEAD THAT HE PLACED UNIQUELY WITHIN EACH HEART!*

In the discovery of the personal love He has for our own lives, let us not assume that we should no longer consider the way of others or even glean from the fruit of their lives. Though He *does* love us in this indescribably individual way, I am nevertheless but one window into His heart, and I enter into knowing Him as I peer through *all* the mysteries He places around me. I

72

must receive both the very personal way that He comes and reveals His love to me and then add to that understanding all that I can glean from the gardens of others.

This is our eternal occupation. Forever, we will be gathering new comprehensions and adding new revelations to this garden as He eternally reveals and unfolds more and more of His beauty and majesty. As He progressively reveals His beauty to us for all the ages to come, we will fall down saying, "Too much, too much!!" Then, with holy craving, we will arise and say, "Never enough! Never enough!" Forever, we will continue this divine exchange of affection.

Personal Love

The Lord reveals Himself to us in many ways. There is the general way that He relates to all of the ones He loves such as through speaking through His Word and revealing His love through others around us. Though He reveals Himself in these collective ways, there is also a specific dimension that He relates to each individual. Just as uniquely as the way He created me is the way that He relates to me, speaks to me and reveals His love to me. He fashioned my frame and knows its frailty. He knows what strengthens me and what hinders me, what delights me and what devastates me.

He knows my frame. On the basis of this perfect knowledge and concentrated love, He interacts with me. He loves the way He made me and does not desire in any way to contradict it but only to enhance it, beautify it and strengthen it. He honors Himself as the Creator by loving His creation in suitable and fitting ways. Though this unique "way" may ebb and flow through the different seasons of my spiritual life, as I look back one day over all of my years, this common thread will reveal itself as God's distinctive expression of His love to my heart.

He honors the way that we receive, the way that we hear and the way that we understand. He loves and agrees with what He created in each one, and as unique as each person is is the uniqueness of how He reveals His love to each individual heart. We must become students of His "way" with us that we might more quickly recognize and receive His affections and leadings. His "way" with me, or the way that He relates to me, flows out of the very specific way that He formed me. Knowing His way with our hearts involves knowing ourselves, with our own personal rhythms and frames. Let us consider this. If He relates to me according to the limitations of my frame and the capacity of my heart and mind, are not those specific details of my person worth studying? And if truly there resides within me a beautiful mystery of Jesus, indeed a very reflection of His heart, and every part of my creation points to it, will I not do well to peer into the way He has formed me—the intricacy of my frame—so that I might discover and understand what He has desired to reveal of Himself within me?

Now this is not an inward search unto a heightened self-knowledge or self-awareness. It is the knowledge of God that we are after. Yet in our search for Him, we must consider what He has hidden within the ones He has created in His image. Let us not neglect to ask Him to reveal what part of His Person He has sought to reveal within our own lives.

Along with this discovering comes the great need for my deep agreement with what He has formed within me. In my creation He declared, "It is good," and His delight was in each detail of my composition. Both the strengths and the weaknesses that He gave me form the fragrance of my beauty, and all must be embraced by my own mind and heart. In this embrace, my soul is calmed and quieted (Ps. 131:2), and I become as one who has found peace before His eyes (Song Sol. 8:10). No longer riding the waves of all the comparisons, I say, "Yes," to the glory He has hidden within me. I begin to love who I am for it is the very design of the Bridegroom Creator. In this deep agreement, I am freed to finally enter the fullness of all that He purposed within me.

Personal Union

His desire is for me. There is an intimacy, a "union" or a "marriage," that only arises from the chamber of my heart. The knowledge of God is different for every heart. Every discovery of God is distinctively portioned and appointed for the person that discovers it and cannot be given away to others. One soul cannot say to another, "Look what I have found in God! Here, take it for your own heart!" For God reveals Himself to one heart according to the intricate details that only Creator knows of creature. Down through all the corridors and crevices of the heart, He makes Himself known in sweet discovery…leaving the soul to always be somewhat alone and separated from others in this revelation…yet forever holding this secret place of communion with its God. In this way, He marries us to Himself in holy union, and no angel or demon, neither life nor death, nor any created thing can separate us from Him.

He is joining our hearts to His in ways never to be fully comprehended or experienced by another. For the same characteristic of God—when woven together with one person, involving that person's individual fashioning, frame, emotional make-up, perceptions and understandings—creates an entirely different reality than another person's encounter with the same quality of God. In this way, He marries Himself to each soul that loves Him, and yet no "marriage" looks the same. Just as in the natural, if one man were to marry two different women during his life, how tremendously dissimilar would his marriages be! Though the same man was husband in each marriage, the qualities and characteristics of the individual unions would be so vastly different. Though God is the same yesterday, today and forever, each soul can only know Him as He reveals Himself to him or her. What one heart finds in Him is so different than what another discovers, yet none less true.

EVERY DISCOVERY OF GOD IS DISTINCTIVELY PORTIONED AND APPOINTED FOR THE PERSON THAT DISCOVERS IT AND CANNOT BE GIVEN AWAY TO OTHERS.

Our Maker is our Husband (Is. 54:5). The One who created is the One who deeply desires. As unique as every snowflake that falls to the ground is every soul that walks the earth. Just as He did not create generically, He does not love generically. Romance would have it no other way. He reveals Himself in one way to one person and in another way to a different person. He is the Husband of every soul that loves Him, and He never tires of awakening each heart with love morning by morning. For one, He paints a sunset; for another, He conducts a thunderstorm. To the heart in need of deliverance, He shows Himself powerful, and to the broken and bruised soul, He shows His immeasurable tenderness.

He spends His days as a Bridegroom, winning the hearts of the bride to Himself. Each intricate revelation that He gives of Himself to the human soul is divine artwork. He does nothing in vain. On the canvas of each soul, He paints His beautiful love. With different colors and diverse shades, He expresses His affections with meticulous skill. Every minute illustration of His affection is the handiwork of God. Every articulation of His love is in itself a masterpiece. With immeasurable care and attention, He weaves each beloved soul to Himself. And thus, all across the earth and throughout all of history we find beautiful, individual, distinctive unions with God, each a unique display of the Master Craftsman, the Creator-Husband.

> *JUST AS HE DID NOT CREATE GENERICALLY, HE DOES NOT LOVE GENERICALLY.*

Personal Way

"...I will go my way to the mountain..." (Song Sol. 4:6).

When the Lord looks upon me with His fiery eyes, He sees only me. I stand alone in His gaze of affection. When He considers me, He does not line me up beside all the other burning hearts that surround me.

He thinks upon me alone and sees only me. He has formed my heart individually and my way, the path before me, uniquely. He measures neither my heart nor my path by that of another. He desires from me what I alone can give Him—the sweet movements of my heart toward Him, the intimacy that I return to Him. He desires intimacy—the kind which He Himself gives my heart to love Him with. And yet one of the greatest hindrances to this sweet communion is when I bring others with me into this garden of intimacy. I so often bring others' giftings, the "favors" the Lord has shown them and even their weaknesses along with me when I come before the Lord in prayer, rendering me unable to be "alone with the Alone."

It is a difficult thing to come before the throne of grace entirely alone in the simplicity of just God and my heart. In so many ways, some conscious, some unaware, I come before Him dragging a collection of other people's attainments or disappointments, strengths and weaknesses. I even bring my perceptions of their intimacy with Jesus before Him as though it directly related to my own. In my emotions, I approach Him as though He were simultaneously thinking of all of these other people when He looks at me. This is partly because of my fear of being alone with Him. I would rather remain in the crowd because I somehow feel safer there. It is also because I

ALL ACROSS THE EARTH AND THROUGHOUT ALL OF HISTORY WE FIND BEAUTIFUL, INDIVIDUAL, DISTINCTIVE UNIONS WITH GOD, EACH A UNIQUE DISPLAY OF THE MASTER CRAFTSMAN, THE CREATOR-HUSBAND.

am so used to living life in the eyes of many instead of the eyes of One. When I live before His eyes alone and not for the approval of others, I can then grasp that I stand alone in His gaze. He awaits me and sees only me when He looks upon me. I cannot know the ways of others and how another's heart ascends into the place of meeting with their God. I can only know my way and movements of this heart. Therefore, why should I any longer bring others into the chamber that was ordained for me alone?

As individually as He has formed each heart, each body, each personality, so the distinctiveness of each one's way in God. In the tapestry of His sovereignty, He has laid out my times and the individual seasons and circumstances to bring me into wholehearted love and the fullness of God for my life. To try to go the way of another only slows our journey for He has formed each one's way for him or her alone. It will not look the way of another. When one is in a season of blessing, another will be in a season of drought. This is an important truth, for we waste much time and emotion comparing our spiritual lives to those around us as though we could be measured by each other.

To try and leave our sovereign season because we see another's as more valuable is a misunderstanding of God's way. Every season has value, and every day is a part of bringing me forward into the fullness He has ordained for me. I must go my own way because that is the only way. There truly is no option except to lose my way. To take the detour of trying another's path is just that, a detour. My heart was made for my way, and that is the pathway into His heart He has laid out for me. He has chosen my way, and it is perfect. There is no flaw in its detail. Yet my "yes" and continual partnering are necessary to reach the final arrival at the ultimate destination chosen for me before there was time.

"The Power of Love's Fullness"

And what if it is true? What if truly the Father and the Son looked at the human race as they sat enthroned in all of their glory. Jesus said, "I will go for her. My longing is too great. I will leave all of My glory. I will leave My throne. I will dress Myself in humanity's clothes and become one of them forever." What if He did come in carpenter's garments all so that she would be His?

And what if it is true that His love is for me, me and me alone? What if truly He would not take another in my place? What if truly there is a place within His heart that my being has come from, a place He has reserved for me alone? What if every human being on the earth and from generations past and to come will never satisfy that specific place that He has named for me?

What if He is really awaiting my love to be awakened? If it were not so, would He not have created many alike, with the same frames, personalities and minds, so that if one would not say, "Yes," another would? But no. It isn't so. Never in all of history has there been another like me. He wouldn't have it. His desire is for me in a way identical to no other (Song Sol. 6:9). Others are irrelevant when it comes to me in His heart. He desires me.

"Enjoy Me"

I think I've been running all day. It seems almost humorous to run when I don't have even an audience or place to run to...like avoiding the only other person in a small room. But I can run no more. I lift my eyes to the Eyes that have held me in their gaze all the day, and I say, "Have me. Enjoy me. Here is my heart. Here is my life. All I have to offer is broken and weak. Have me, Jesus. Enjoy me.

Oh Jesus, truly I can only whisper a prayer. My heart is faint. My pain is real. I feel that yesterday's prayers had more life than these, and yesterday's seemed so dry and weak. But even so, I cry out Your name. Jesus! You are the Lifter of my head. You are the Sustainer of my soul. Surely, You will see me through this day and cause me to come up smiling.

CHAPTER 6

DARK YET LOVELY

"Dark am I, yet lovely, O daughters of Jerusalem, dark like the tents of Kedar, like the tent curtains of Solomon" (Song Sol. 1:5, NIV).

It had been a bitter, lonely day in prayer as my sister Deborah searched the Word to find that nothing seemed alive and searched her own heart to find that nothing seemed to move. Only stillness. Only silence. Only a lonely apartment and a barren soul. The Word seemed so dry and empty. Instead of feeling tender love for the Lord, only a gnawing ache of loneliness arose from within. Every argument raised its voice, and every place of weakness made itself known. All outward and inward beauties seemed to vanish, leaving only darkness. His "fiery affections" seemed far. A life of prayer seemed foolish though just yesterday it seemed so immensely wise and enjoyable. Pacing…sitting…searching the Word…praying out loud…silence. Which was worse—the pain of His silence or the disillusionment of her love's weakness? It was all she could do to stay and continue instead of reaching for something to "prop up" her soul and deliver her from this place of barrenness. Ruined for comforts and pleasures once fulfilling yet experiencing nothing of the sweetness desired in communion, she remained trapped before her silent Beloved. Waiting in the silence…despairing of soul…empty…alone.

After a day in its entirety, when her mind and emotions were spent, it seemed that the best option was to give up and go to bed. Yet as she laid there in the darkness, one last cry arose from her heart. She lifted her arms wide to the Lord and said with all of her strength and love, "Enjoy me. Right here, right now, in my absolute weakness, enjoy me." For the first time all day, something broke within, and instant tears flooded from her heart as she felt the Lord bestow honor upon her in this place of deepest weakness. As she presented her great emptiness, He flooded her with dignity, embracing her weak places and crowning her with His enjoyment. This exchange so transformed her that she has not ever been the same. As she drank of His enjoyment in her lowest place of weakness, something profound happened within the inner regions of her soul. She received the spirit of grace and beauty in that place and experienced one of the most powerful rewards of the gospel.

Like the maiden in the Song of Solomon, we begin our journey of bridal love with a crucial revelation. And He brings us here quite purposefully through the

> *SHE LIFTED HER ARMS WIDE TO THE LORD AND SAID WITH ALL OF HER STRENGTH AND LOVE, "ENJOY ME. RIGHT HERE, RIGHT NOW, IN MY ABSOLUTE WEAKNESS, ENJOY ME."*

help of our own immaturity. Though sincere desire for Jesus burns within us, we unavoidably run headlong into our own weakness. Our passion for Him is real. Our sincerity is sure. Yet we lack spiritual maturity. We cannot go long before we discover our utter inability to sustain our fervency. It is when we encounter this insufficiency that He reveals the paradox of His grace and we declare, "I am dark yet lovely." Before anything else on the journey, we encounter this absolutely necessary truth. He reveals to us that even in our weakness and immaturity we are beautiful to Him because of the resounding "yes" towards Him within our heart. We possess weak flesh but a willing spirit (Matt 26:41). The reality of our sin and shortcomings does not keep us from the experience of His enjoyment. For even in this place He calls us lovely by our sincerity of desire and wholehearted pursuit of Him. We come to understand that the very presence of genuine aspiration to obey Jesus is the beginning of our spiritual victory.

A Paradox of Grace

We are on a journey to wholehearted Love. Our desire is to reach the fullness of Love and all that God would give to the human heart according to the riches of the glory of His inheritance in us (Eph. 1:18). Yet before we take even one step forward, Jesus speaks this foundational fact to each believer's heart. He reveals the reality that we are unmistakably, unavoidably dark. Some of this darkness is actual sin and compromise that must be rooted out of our lives as we come into agreement with His love. And some of our darkness is but the weakness of our fallenness only to be reversed in the age to come. Yet as we see this darkness, He reveals that we are also *lovely* to Him even in the process of our growth and maturity in Love. He possesses pleasure in us while we are moving from strength to strength (Ps. 84:7) and from glory to glory (2 Cor. 3: 18).

To know that I am *dark yet lovely* is to understand my weakness, which is comprised of my sinfulness, my immaturity and my natural limitations *together with* the revelation of my loveliness to Him. David expresses this twofold mystery in Psalm 86, "Bow down Your ear, O Lord, hear me; for I *am poor and needy*. Preserve my life for I *am holy*..." (1-2, emphasis added).

When He gazes upon me, instead of seeing only that which has fully come into maturity, He perceives the yet-maturing virtues within me. He hears my inward cries to fully belong to Him. When I stumble in my persistent weakness, His gaze pierces through my external struggle and sees, in my spirit, the internal flame of true yearning to be His. With His eyes of fire, He perceives the continual cry deep within my heart to belong fully to Him, and He calls it part of my "loveliness." He defines me by the things that are not yet revealed as though they were. When I lie on my bed at night and long for victory in my weak areas, He esteems my longing precious and receives my cry.

We must accurately perceive how God thinks about us in our weakness. He's a God of unending kindness, and His mercy is not challenged by our lack. That Jesus could be filled with love and enjoyment in someone when he or she is still stumbling and immature seems unrighteous or unjust to our false understandings of Him. We imagine that this kind of affection is possible only when we are fully pure, holy and mature. Yet the glorious good news of all time is that Jesus, the perfect One, set His affections on those who were fully weak and undeserving. While we were still His enemies, He died for us, and while we are yet immature, He enjoys us. This isn't to say He enjoys sin but that He delights in the lover of God who is yet in the struggle against besetting sins.

We are far weaker than we realize and far lovelier than we realize, and yet even in our greatest weakness God perceives in us more beauty than we can imagine. Our loveliness is not an attribute gained by our attainments. It is a gift of God. He sees us beautiful because of what He Himself has accomplished in our salvation and transformation. This divine perspective is our source of protection from the accusations of the enemy. When the accuser seeks to poison me with accusation regarding my weakness or immaturity, I respond with the truth of Jesus' delight in me even in my weakness. When He comes to deceive me into taking pride in my beauty or strength, I respond with the vivid remembrance of my weakness.

Without this combined confession, our darkness and our loveliness, we cannot continually ascend in our journey of His embrace. This paradox must live within our hearts. We never let go of this two-part revelation in this life for its combination protects our hearts as we make our way forward in love. Our loveliness protects us from shame and condemnation, and our weakness keeps us from pride and arrogance. Both of them work together for our good. They enable us to wholeheartedly abandon ourselves in love, remaining confident before Him and continuing with boldness in our pursuit of knowing Him. In the age to come, we will marvel at how this twofold revelation anchored and centered us. As we stand in our perfected glory, our hearts will overflow with gratitude at God's genius displayed in the way He married weakness and strength within the human heart's ascent out of the brokenness of a fallen world into the excellent beauty of the everlasting Kingdom.

The Beauty of Our Wholehearted Pursuit

We are dark yet lovely. We are weak yet enjoyed. And this divine enjoyment over the life of a believer is not stagnant. It comes in the midst of a movement, of a godly struggle and a holy pursuit. The enjoyment of God comes as we fiercely seek to overcome those weak areas of sin and compromise in our lives through the power of His love. It is in the context of while we are yet struggling and warring against the enemies of God in our personal lives that He empowers us with the reality of His pleasure in us. His delight does not come when sin is tolerated but when righteousness is fervently sought after.

It is in the context of our wholehearted pursuit of Him that His enjoyment finds us. Even when we fail utterly and stumble miserably in this pursuit, His pleasure over us is not diminished. Yet this pleasure of God cannot be separated from our sincerity of heart. To say that He enjoys me while I tolerate sin and darkness is a severe untruth. To the one who fears Him, He will give a thousand graces and mercy unending. Yet to the one who presumes upon His grace and harbors compromise and darkness, He sets Himself as an adversary.

As we grow in the understanding of His mercy and grace, we must keep within our remembrance not only His kindness but His severity (Rom. 11:22). These are the heights and depths of His Person. His kindness is unending, and His jealousy is unyielding. We gain great confidence in knowing the kindness and mercy of God in the midst of our weakness. And God wills it to be so. He created us to be without blame before Him in love (Eph. 1:4). Yet coupled with His tenderness and without any contradiction is His zeal for the total possession of our lives.

WE HAVE A GOD OF SEVERE ZEAL FOR THE ENTIRE LORDSHIP OF OUR HEARTS. HE IS NOT A GOD OF FRACTIONS BUT OF FULLNESS.

We have a God of severe zeal for the entire lordship of our hearts. He is not a God of fractions but of fullness. He is a jealous God (Ex. 34:14). He desires us completely and utterly. This jealousy flows harmoniously and without opposition to His mercy. In His zeal, He unyieldingly resists the one who knowingly tolerates secret sin and compromise, but in His tenderness, He gives immeasurable grace to the one who fears Him and stands sincere before Him in love. "Or do you think that the Scripture says in vain, 'The Spirit who dwells in us yearns jealously'? But He gives more grace. Therefore He says: 'God resists the proud but gives grace to the humble'" (James 4:5-6).

It is the one who is in this wholehearted pursuit of Him, fleeing darkness and pursuing light, that He calls lovely. All along the journey, through all the processes of maturing, He views that one as beautiful and pleasing. He sees as man does not see and determines success by standards we have not conceived. What man calls miserable, He calls beautiful, and what man deems small God knows as mighty. He is Himself beauty, and thus His definitions of beauty are the only ones true. What He calls lovely is indeed lovely though all the earth may disagree.

Let us now look into just what He perceives when He calls one on the earth "lovely" to His beholding.

Receiving the Truth of my Beauty

The beauty of a believer's heart before Him flows from an entire wellspring of sources. The first source is God Himself. It is the very ocean of His personality. Because of the heart of the Beholder, we are beautiful to God, and His view of people flows out of the River of Pleasures that abides in His own heart. "For the Lord takes pleasure in His people..." (Ps. 149:4). Even from creation, His heart has swelled with eternal pleasure, and from that pleasure, He has taken delight in what He has formed in mankind, calling it good. "Then I was beside Him as a master craftsman; and I was daily His delight, rejoicing always before Him, rejoicing in His inhabited world, and my delight was with the sons of men" (Prov. 8:30-31).

I have already mentioned that the beauty of the believer's heart is a gift from God. This gift is salvation. Our loveliness before Him streams from the righteousness that our Beloved purchased for us in His death on the cross. "For He made Him who knew no sin to be sin for us, that we might become the righteousness of God in Him" (2 Cor. 5:21). Out of Himself flows salvation, and out of His pleasure and desire for people He beautifies His enemies with salvation. By the labors of His soul and not by anything that we have done, He has wrapped us in His own beautiful garments. "...He will beautify the humble with salvation" (Ps. 149:4).

The willing spirit He gave each one of us at the new birth is yet another source of His enjoyment over us. This is the "yes" in our spirit before we have ever changed anything outwardly. "...The spirit indeed is willing, but the flesh is weak" (Matt. 26:41). The Lord looks at the heart of man and perceives our movement toward Him before it is even externally evident.

Besides all of these glorious realities, His pleasure in us also flows from the eternal torrent of our destiny as the future bride of God's Beloved Son. In other words, He is totally committed to giving His Son an equally yoked partner in love and He possesses great delight in the one He is so committed to bring forth. "For Zion's sake I will not hold My peace, and for Jerusalem's sake I will not rest, until her righteousness goes forth as brightness, and her salvation as a lamp that burns" (Is. 62:1). We are His inheritance, and within us He shall see the labor of His soul and be satisfied (Is. 53:11). Forever, we will be an adorned and enthroned bride in the embrace of the Lamb of God. Oh, how lovely we are to Him! Oh, how beautiful even now are we before His gaze!! The cherished lovely one and the desired chosen beloved of the King eternal.

A very real and necessary part of our journey is receiving this loveliness and His enjoyment in our darkest place. It is not enough to know His enjoyment and delight in me in my strengths or on my good days. For the moment that I encounter my weakness, I am dismayed and assume that I am disqualified. To consistently grow spiritually requires this revelation that we are lovely to God while we are in the process of discovering the darkness of our own heart. When we spread our arms wide open to Him while we are covered with the shadows of our weakness, the transforming power and glory of redemption breaks into our dark places and begins to enlighten our broken understandings of His nature. We begin to recognize that our loveliness to Him is not based on our success or failure but on His own definition. We begin to be rooted and grounded in the love of Christ (Eph. 3:17).

The Beauty of the Heart's Opening

In my own journey, I have greatly witnessed this principle of being enjoyed while yet in weakness through the crowning glory of my life—my husband Matthew. I have the very rare honor of being married to an earthly bridegroom who from the beginning has locked arms with the Heavenly Bridegroom and said, "Jesus, how can we romance and win her heart?" What an overwhelming position it is to be on the other side of that united pursuit!! I remember the pain of some of the first times Matt saw the "darkness" of my heart. I think I had a subconscious goal of staying perfect before his eyes and not ever letting my faults be revealed. So my first response was to cover my weakness and keep him from knowing what was really there. I didn't want to expose the dark places within my heart to him for fear that he would love me less or see me differently.

I remember one of these times when my emotions felt pretty dark, fleshly and sinful. I didn't want to express my feelings to my husband because of their ungodliness. I was hoping to just avoid the subject until I could somehow get out of the gloomy hole I was in. He asked me, "What are you feeling? Tell me what's going on in your heart." As I hesitated and tried to avoid his questions, he said a profound thing that I've never forgotten. He said, "Dana, it's not the substance of what you make known to me that's beautiful; it's the opening of your heart. It is the 'yes' in your heart to be mine. The fact that you are revealing the secrets and letting me peer into your heart—that is in itself the beautiful part."

Our Eternal Bridegroom receives us even far beyond this natural reflection. He places dignity and value upon the very reach of our hearts to belong fully to Him. He calls it a "willing spirit." He sees tremendous beauty in our choice to move toward Him in the times when we would rather run and hide because of our darkness. He deems this choice most beautiful and pleasing and sees past our current scope of weakness to the distant horizon of mature love, shining in its full strength.

This is so contradictory to what we expect of Him. It runs cross-grain with what we believe He is like. We imagine Him to be grieved, disappointed and reluctant to receive us while we are yet so stained. The hardest thing for us to do in these times is to lift up our brokenness to His piercing gaze and stand just as we are before Him. Our proneness is to shrink away from Him in shame, imagining that even He would prefer it that way. We tell ourselves that we cannot approach Him until we have put things in order and again feel worthy of His affection. All the while He is looking at us with a steady gaze that beckons, *"Open your heart to Me. I know your flesh is weak, but I am moved with love by your willing spirit. The opening of your heart, the very movement toward Me as you are faced with your weakness is most lovely to Me."*

OUR AGREEMENT WITH HIS LOVE WHILE WE ARE YET MATURING IS THE GREAT CLIMAX OF OUR SALVATION JOURNEY.

It is a sign of truly comprehending the heart of our Beloved when we reach for His love from the pit of our darkness. When we take this risk, we demonstrate our confidence in the strength of His love and the certainty of His enjoyment. Not until we have exercised this *reach* will we begin to drink of the deepest wells of salvation. Our agreement with His love while we are yet maturing is the great climax of our salvation journey. When I open my heart to him, regardless of the substance within, I stand in my true position of bridal intimacy, receiving the true work of redemption.

Out of jealousy for Him and my jealousy that I would be His, I rise up as His chosen bride and receive my inheritance of His delight in me. This is *my part* for He is not the only One who carries jealousy for our union. I arise and cry out, "I am Yours, and I will share with You all that is in my heart. I *will* be Yours." In doing this, I partner with Him in the conquering of my own heart. I boldly run into the throne room of grace, throwing open my arms and saying, "Here I am, the one that You love! Enjoy me!"

Unnecessary Distance

How many countless hours have I wasted distancing myself from the One who loves me? Growing up, I remember sitting in church each week and evaluating my position before Him. I measured where I was with God according to how much time I had spent with Him and what good things I had done to please Him in the last few days. If I felt successful in both of these categories, I approached Him with confidence and boldness. If I failed my self-evaluation, which was much more often, I would distance my heart from Him for many hours and days until I could acquire enough on my "good works list" to permit me access. I would pray, "God, I cannot face you right now. I'll go to the meeting and sit in the crowd, but I can't come near to You until I feel clean enough and deserving of Your presence. Until then I will remain here and endure this distance."

On one side of our false measurements is the feeling of success based on untrue terms. We allow ourselves nearness to Him based upon wrong ideas about why we are permitted access to Him. When we feel we're successful because of how much time we have spent with Him or all the good things we have done for Him, we build up our faulty foundation and feed our false ideas about His character and about our saving redemption in Him alone. We come near because we feel we have done it right and our works have measured up. On the other side, when we come up against the reality of our own weakness and sin, we create a one-sided distance in our relationship while we turn and try to clean ourselves up or cover our faults with good works. We try to bring our own accomplishments to the table as though the triumph of His cross were not enough.

When we stumble in our spiritual journey, we easily lose sight of the full acceptance and *enjoyment* God has for us even in the midst of our weakness. We determine our nearness to Him by a false evaluation system and we deny ourselves the gift of what His blood already paid for in redemption. The truth is that He does not receive me nor deny me access to His presence based on my own righteousness but always on the foundation of the cross and redemption. Clothed in His own righteousness, I am given continuous free access to His throne of grace so that I might come boldly before Him with full confidence and complete assurance. I am set free by the blood of Jesus, and I can bring nothing to the table to motivate the heart of God into the response of forgiveness. He desires me by His own self-replenishing love that exists within Himself, unaltered by my response.

In these crises experiences, we so often allow ourselves the legal position of salvation yet deny ourselves intimacy with Him. Intimacy seems too pleasurable for what we deserve. We assume that His enjoyment is an exclusive reward for the mature and holy and that we can only know intimacy when we are worthy of it. We somehow imagine that we are doing

God a favor to sit in our penalty box until we have
served our time and paid the price for our stumbling.
We keep ourselves distant from Him and allow our
hearts to become emotionally paralyzed before Him.

Though we know the cross is about forgiveness
of sin, we neglect its provision for Christ's intimacy
with believers who still
struggle with sin. The
power of redemption was
its glorious ripping away
of the veil between the
weak and the Great High
Priest. He tore the veil in
two that I might approach
Him freely without hin-
drance. To deny ourselves intimacy with Him is to deny
ourselves the power of redemption. He paid the price
for my sin that I might forever live in His embrace. He
made a way for me to forever be joined to Him as His
eternal partner, the adorned, embraced and enthroned
bride of the Lamb.

To keep myself at a distance is more than unnec-
essary; it is sin and one of Satan's most subtle ways of
stealing from our hearts. When we do this, we agree
with the lie that our weakness is greater than Jesus'
work of redemption, and we stand in the way of God
Himself by counting our own evaluation of our hearts
higher than His. We offer Him no favors to distance
ourselves from Him, rather we deny Him the nearness
that His blood paid for. He is a Bridegroom, who out
of great zeal and desire for His bride, came to the earth
and purchased our position as His eternal partner. He

> *THOUGH WE KNOW THE
> CROSS IS ABOUT
> FORGIVENESS OF SIN, WE
> NEGLECT ITS PROVISION
> FOR CHRIST'S INTIMACY
> WITH BELIEVERS WHO
> STILL STRUGGLE WITH SIN.*

deeply desires that we would approach Him with boldness because of our position in grace and because of the raging fire of love within His heart toward us as His longed for bride.

He desires that we come to Him as we are, bringing nothing except the glorious work of salvation and the riches of redemption. He wrapped us in the robes of righteousness—the same beautiful garments that Jesus possesses. When we encounter our weakness, we can lift up our voices with hearts of gratitude and say, "Here I am! The one that You love! Here is Your favorite one!" Instead of distancing ourselves in shame and accusation, we stand in the truth of who we are by the blood of the Lamb. With confident hearts, we cry out with the psalmist, "What shall I render to the Lord for all of His benefits toward me? I will take up the cup of salvation, and call upon the name of the Lord. I will pay my vows to the Lord now in the presence of all the people" (Ps. 116:12-14). And with amazing love He responds, "You are so beautiful to Me! Though you are broken and weak, I see you as radiant because of My Son's garments of righteousness that I have wrapped you in."

In the place of my utter weakness, when I feel the weight of its strength, the enemy would have me to believe that it is too great for Jesus' delight to still call me lovely. He would lead me to imagine that my weakness has disqualified me. I am the uniquely dark one, who is exempt from God's delight and enjoyment. In these times, I picture my sin and my weakness so dark. I imagine the depths of their pit and how far they descend. But then as I come to the bottom, there I see the

Lamb of God, Jesus Christ. He is beneath, even up-holding them upon Himself. There is no place of weakness or sin that He has not descended lower than. There is no uniquely dark one exempt from the gift of redemption. There is no lover of God who carries weakness lower than He has already descended.

My weak heart is beautiful to God. I am embraced and enjoyed even in weakness. I am loved, adored, cherished and desired even now. It's who I am. Even as I am making my way forward in love, with immaturity so often lifting its head, He sees the sweet budding desire in my heart and calls me lovely. This is my confidence and my song whenever I discover my weakness. We enter into one of the most powerful mysteries of redemption when we begin to touch this reality. The person that feels loved and pure, overflowing with dignity and desire, is fearless and tenacious in love. So few ever touch this profound place of dignity, but those that do are the mighty ones in the earth. They are the burning and shining lamps throughout history that triumph over the enemies of their soul and walk in the truth of their destiny.

As He leads our hearts along on this journey, carrying this paradox of grace within, one of the first introductions He gives us is the taste of longing for more of Himself. It is not an all together foreign taste for we have known it as long as we have walked this earth. Yet in the realm of this freshly awakened love, how new and sharp it feels within our souls. He is reintroducing us to the companion we will grow to know so well in all of the journey ahead.

"Heart Ache"

Aching Heart and longing soul,
Waiting for my Love.
Trying not to find despair
But to cling to Eternal Hope.
O Jesus, Fair and Beautiful.
O Sweet Lover so Divine.
My heart, my heart, my aching heart
Only wishes to be Thine.
Do You hold me as You promised?
Do You keep me as You said?
Will oceans never separate us?
Will my longings soon be met?
Longing, my food, tears, my drink,
I search my skies for You.
I wait, I wait, and more I wait.
My Beloved will be true.
Do not be far, O hurtful thought.
Come quickly to my soul.
Let rain fall, let light shine,
Delay not to make me whole.
My Beloved mine and I am His.
Oh, for His embrace.
By night I dream, by day I watch
For one glimpse of glorious Face.
Aching heart and longing soul,
The only offerings mine to give.
I ask only for Thyself
For this alone I live.

Chapter 7

Longing

"Father, I DESIRE that they also whom You gave Me may be with Me where I am, that they may behold My glory which You have given Me..." (Jn. 17:24, emphasis added).

To begin the subject of the great longing ever-present within love, we must start with *the longing of God,* who is Love Himself. For surely we long because He longs, and any desire for Him that we experience may find its reference point within His own heart. Ours is a God who is wounded with love for human beings. "For the Lord's portion is His people" (Deut. 32:9). Somewhere in the depths of God's being, He has reserved room for this ordained desire. His is not a longing that arises from need or lack. The One who is *Love* does not love out of absence but out of *presence.* His longing is not about filling a place where He is incomplete but about bringing those He loves into the fullness of His embrace. The Creator desires to bring the created into the communion shared between Father, Son and Holy Spirit. His determined desire is to bring us into the plentitude of love within the Godhead.

When Jesus spoke, "'Father, I desire that they would be with Me where I am,'" He affirmed the ever-present desire of God from eternity—that humanity would be brought near to Him, entering into the fellowship of the Godhead. In His everlasting kindness, He has willed that we would be with Him where He is: the dwelling place of His eternal love. Yet He will not force us into this fellowship. He waits to be wanted. He longs that we would long for Him. He makes room for the voice of our choice.

> HE WAITS TO BE WANTED. HE LONGS THAT WE WOULD LONG FOR HIM. HE MAKES ROOM FOR THE VOICE OF OUR CHOICE.

With His wounded heart of love, He is searching for something He has positioned Himself not to have unless we choose to give it to Him. "'Yet a time is coming and has now come when the true worshipers will worship the Father in spirit and truth, for they are the kind of worshipers the Father seeks'" (Jn. 4:23, NIV). He is searching for worshipers. He is seeking voluntary lovers. For this, He longs. For this, He thirsts. His eyes search to and fro to find the hearts who keep His covenant of love (2 Chron. 16:9). He desires that we would join Him in the realm of love where He lives by allowing our own hearts to be caught up in this eternal divine desire.

Echoes of Divine Love

Every yearning for God we ever experience is encompassed within the Great Desire of our God. If the reality of Jesus' "Father I Desire" were a chamber, we would find each one of our own desires for God holding residence within that chamber. We desire God because He first desired us. We long because He longs. Every desire we have for Him is not from our own heart but from His. We are created in His image, and we desire Him because He has caused us to be caught up within the flaming desire in His own heart.

To long for God is to say, "Yes," to the invitation of participation in the desire of God. If every longing that we have for Him can find its origin in His own heart, then to long for Him is only to join Him in His own desire. Our desire for Him is but a partaking of His own desire. When we enter into our inheritance of longing for God, we are only participating and engaging in what has always resided within His heart. Our hearts come into agreement and alignment with His.

He is both the Longing and the Fulfillment of Love. The One who is Desire is also the One who is Satisfaction. Within Him is the wound and the healing. In as much as our hunger can be traced back to Him, so can our filling. He provides the thirst that makes us desperate, and He provides the drink that satisfies. We partake of His longing, and we partake of His fulfillment. He desires that we would be with Him in love and union, satisfied forever in the eternal pleasure of His being. Therefore, He brings us into this place of His own longing where we join Him in this divine desire. We long to be with Him where He is. Our hearts cry out, "O God! I must have more of You! I must know You even as I am known!"

HE IS BOTH THE LONGING AND THE FULFILLMENT OF LOVE.

And with each voice of our longing heart is found an echo of God's own heart. We are only desiring what He first desired. We are standing within that chamber of His great longing and drinking of the river of desire present there. "Father, I desire." Surely, He will answer us. If all of our longings are given of God and from His own heart, will He not give us the fulfillment of Himself? If He is the Desire, will He not also be the Satisfier? If He is the Thirst, will He not also be the Water?

The Gift of Longing

After spending many hours before Him one night, I left the Friday night "Watch of the Lord" sulking in discouragement. Once again, He had not come as I desired Him to. As I got into my car, anxious tears freely streaming down my face, a dear friend came up to my window. I voiced my pain that I desired the Lord so much, and yet He still was not revealing Himself to me. To my surprise, she smiled. She leaned in and whispered, "It's happening. You love Him! You love Him so much you weep for Him. Your heart is moving in love just like you've been praying for." Her unexpected angle of discernment struck me. I thought of the prayer I liked to pray over and over again throughout the day, *"Cause this heart to love You. Cause this heart to love You."* Suddenly, I realized that my longing was His answering of my requests. My tears were *love* for Him, the very thing I had been asking for. I loved Him by longing for Him. My heart was beginning to actually move in love, to be tenderized in love and to feel love for my Beloved rising within.

Our journey begins with longing. And before longing is the longing to long. It is the yearning to desire Him. We find in our hearts an awakening that *beckons* longing and paves the way for desire. It begins with the Lord Himself placing His divine drawing upon the heart of the one who loves Him. We find ourselves desiring to desire Him and pained by the present shallowness of our hearts. He awakens us to the great obsession of Himself, and we find this new ache within our hearts: our lack of love and absence of tenderness. We begin to hunger for the capacity to hunger. We begin to thirst for the ability to thirst. The longing to long is the escort into longing itself. It is the God-ordained gateway into the true gift of God to crave Him with all of our beings.

To long for God is to give witness to the Transcendent One. Longing is the echo of eternity within our souls. It is that which sets us apart and makes us pilgrims on the journey. This world is not our home, and our inner ache gives testimony to the brevity of life and the weight of eternity. "I am a stranger in the earth; do not hide Your commandments from me. My soul breaks with longing for your judgments..." (Ps. 119:19-20). Something within us reaches for One who is other than and for a realm that is beyond. We long for One whom we have not yet seen but we love (1 Pet. 1:8). With hearts empowered by a divine ache, we cry out for more of God. We search for any sign of Him. This is

OUR JOURNEY BEGINS WITH LONGING. AND BEFORE LONGING IS THE LONGING TO LONG.

the precise position that He wants us to be in. It is the
hungry that He fills. It is the desirous that He satisfies.
All divine longing is a gift. It takes God to love
God, and He Himself must place within us the love
with which to love Him with. "...For it is God who
works in you both to will [desire]
and to do for His good pleasure"
(Phil. 2:13). Longing is the beginning of that gift of love. We
imagine this gift to be only the
actual *experience* of intimacy with
Him. Part of the actual knowledge or experience of Him in
intimacy is the longing for that experience. The longing
prior to the felt-experience is just as much a part of
loving Him as the experience itself. They go hand in
hand and cannot be separated. The initial longing is an
irreplaceable part of the eternal intimacy. Both the
craving and the satisfaction are equal parts of the gift
of intimacy. It all plays a role in the impartation of
Divine Love to our hearts. Oh, the gift of longing for
God! Oh, treasured companion on the journey! For
surely we need this Helper for the entirety of our way
forward in love. Longing and our ache for His greater
revealing are here to stay.

*BOTH THE
CRAVING AND THE
SATISFACTION ARE
EQUAL PARTS OF
THE GIFT OF
INTIMACY.*

Love's Delay

*"Tell me, O you whom I love, where do you feed Your flock,
where you make it rest at noon. For why should I be as one
who veils herself by the flocks of your companions?"* (Song
Sol. 1:7).

In Song of Solomon 1:7, the young maiden inquires of the Lord where He feeds His flock. She has just told the Lord in verse two that His love is better than wine. She knows His love far exceeds all other pleasures. Her whole life vision has changed because of this foundational revelation. Yet the mere acknowledgement of His love's superiority is not what will ultimately satisfy her hungry heart. Though she has been overcome with the vision of His great love, her heart is still hungry to actually experience it. Only He *Himself* can answer the craving in her soul. She must personally partake of His love in order to find satisfaction. She must *drink* in order for her thirst to be quenched. She asks with desperation, "Tell me where can I go to drink of You; where do I feast upon this love?"

She is saying, "Where do You cause my heart to be satisfied with You and You alone? How is it that a soul drinks deeply of You? For now I am ruined for lesser pleasures. You are my Reward. Now I know that You are exceedingly broad. Who can know the vastness of Your personality? I know that there is more to You than I can fathom or imagine. You are an Ocean, and I stand gazing from the shore. I have been ruined by an awakening, but now my pain is greater than before. The high vision is before me, but I know only hunger and desperation as my reality."

She had not anticipated a delay in experiencing the pleasures of His love. She gave her wholehearted "yes" to the life vision of holy passion yet now finds herself in an unexpected quiet. Here she waits, ruined for lesser pleasures and kept from Divine consolations, in the boundless space between her passion and the beautiful experience of His. He is cultivating longing in her heart. He desires more than a recognition of His greatness; He wants a desperation and lovesick yearning to come to maturity within her. And so for a time she remains in this breach between the *reach* and the *fulfillment* of superior pleasures. She is ruined by the vision of His beauty. She now knows He is altogether lovely and that no other pursuit will ever satisfy the deep cravings of her heart. Yet He keeps her here in this Divine delay for a season and she only knows the ache of longing and not the pleasure of its answer. She only knows the wound of love and not the actual experience of His healing cure.

Desire: the Prelude to Satisfaction Realized

To every heart set on this journey of love comes seasons of great pain due to an awakened heart not yet answered. God awakens longing for Himself within us and then very purposely delays the satisfaction of that longing. Our hearts find an all new thirst, and we begin to burn with the holy expectation of His coming to us to quench what He Himself has slain us with. No longer contented by any other pleasure, we cry out for what we are certain He will impart to us: eternal love from His heart. Yet, instead of divine satisfaction, we find greater heartache. We find ourselves caught in that great chasm between longing and fulfillment. Instead of songs, we find silence. Instead of encounters with our Lord, we find Him seemingly more absent than before.

Understanding God's own longing keeps us from hurt and offense at the Lord when He does not immediately answer the pain of our heartache. Our proneness is to think that God must not understand the pain of our desire when He does not answer us immediately. When we do not understand that our longing originated in His own heart, we are prone to believe that He has left us alone in this painful delay out of a lack of sympathy for our suffering state. Our misunderstandings tell us that if He *did* know the pain we were in, He surely could not bear to leave us in it. Quite the contrary, when we trace our longing back to its source, we find the wounded-by-love heart of God. It is from the deep of His heart that our own deep groans come forth. He knows that without longing we cannot enter into the fullness of His love, and therefore, in His absolute kindness and jealousy over us, He places within us this dagger of desire for Himself.

WE MUST ENCOUNTER THE DEPTHS OF LONGING'S ACHE IN ORDER TO ASCEND TO THE HEIGHTS OF DIVINE EXHILARATION.

These periods of unfulfilled longing are inexpressibly necessary to our journey of love. Of what worth is water without thirst? Of what value is fruitfulness without barrenness? What is desire satisfied without desire unmet? How our hearts need to go hungry before we are fed. We must encounter the depths of longing's ache in order to ascend to the heights of divine exhilaration. He carves us out and enlarges our capacity through hunger and desire that He might fill us with Himself.

When we are flooded with the pain of unan-
swered desire, we often forget that this Divine wound
originated in His heart and not our own. We view our
pain as the absence of God's answer instead of the
presence of it. God does not give Himself except to the
hungry and destitute of heart, yet we cannot produce
hunger for God. It is He Himself who causes hunger to
arise and the prayer for fulfillment to emerge. He
establishes in us the desire that He
intends to satisfy. As surely as the
pain of our longing is the certainty
of His coming to us. When we
begin to feel our own hearts moving in desire and in a painful reach
for God, we may rest assured that
He will answer us. Where there is
Divine longing, there is Divine
fulfillment. Though they may be
separated by a time gap, the two are so interwoven and
undividable that you cannot experience one without
soon knowing the other.

A DIVINELY IMPLANTED DESIRE IS NOTHING SHORT OF A DIVINE PROMISE OF THE VERY THING WE YEARN FOR.

When we begin to cry out to know Him and experience Him in deeper ways, we should not be surprised when He answers us by wounding us with greater
longing. It has always been His way. In fact, we may
look at these desires from Him as promises. For He is
the Inflictor of longing's wound, and He alone can cure
us. A Divinely implanted desire is nothing short of a
Divine promise of the very thing we yearn for. When
we see this as the true beginnings of Love's working its
way into our soul, we will not so quickly lose heart in

the aridity of longing's throws but instead find comfort in the truth that His answer has begun within us.

If we are not careful, we will misinterpret these times and possibly deny some of the greatest fruits to be born in the realm of intimacy. These seasons make a way for the seasons that we crave most. Though they appear to us as brick walls blocking our way forward, they are indeed doorways into greater love. Behind these periods of dryness is the flaming heart of the God-Man who refuses to have a bride not stricken with lovesick desire. For what is a bride without a longing and thirsting heart? His strategic delays are all about awakening love within us. He opens our eyes with a vision of His beauty and then steps back just out of our reach so that sincere longing might be cultivated within us. He prepares the way for a greater revelation of Himself by setting in place the desire that will be its prelude.

HE PREPARES THE WAY FOR A GREATER REVELATION OF HIMSELF BY SETTING IN PLACE THE DESIRE THAT WILL BE ITS PRELUDE.

The Dry Side of Love

To the seeking heart, longing is often mistaken for emptiness—the pervasive feeling. We touch these places of frustration where the barrenness within us is crying out to be filled. Because we don't feel sweetness, as we think longing should feel, we assume that our hearts are only dry and unfruitful. We feel we can't even "long" for God. *Yet one of longing's most common faces is emptiness. It is the dry side of desire and the empty side of love.* There is no sweetness about it—only raw barrenness lifting its voice. This frigid form of longing is yet indeed longing though it is a lovesickness devoid of swooning and thick with the frustration of dissatisfied desire. When longing comes in its dry attire, we so often do not recognize it, and we lose heart very quickly. Yet we must learn to recognize this face of longing and receive it with an open heart, just as we would if it came with tears and sweet tenderness.

The hardest days have always been the days without tears, for tears are the outer proof of the inner workings. Without them, I am left alone with a void of emotion, and I question my own heart much more aggressively. It is a risky thing to believe that the reason we are not feeling the presence of the Lord is because He is awakening love in us by hiding Himself. Is it not easier to believe I have grieved Him, and thus He has withdrawn His presence from me? How quickly am I willing to blame myself for these delays, as if they were not supposed to be part of my spiritual calendar and only emerged because of some fault of my own.

ONE OF LONGING'S MOST COMMON FACES IS EMPTINESS. IT IS THE DRY SIDE OF DESIRE AND THE EMPTY SIDE OF LOVE.

How many a day have I pained over my silent heart? Without knowing how to recognize longing, I believed my heart to be a silent tomb incapable of flowing as a river of love. If we do not have an understanding of this arid side of longing, we will write off many a day for "wasted" when indeed it was rich with love. Instead, we must comfort our hearts by focusing on *His* perspective of our days not our own. A bleak and silent day before Him rises to *Heaven* as one filled with sweet melodies of love and the kind of fragrance that can only be acquired through the pressure of heartache.

Often times, what we behold as dry is truly a fountain in the eyes of the Eternal One. We gage so much on emotion, or the lack thereof, yet love cannot be measured by what is *felt*. So often our moments of greatest love come out of the places of greatest dryness and barrenness. We set our will and choose love when no emotion or feeling comes to our aid. I believe that these will be the moments that Jesus brings to our remembrance when we stand before Him face to face one day. He will reveal to us the most hidden workings of our hearts in these times when all we were aware of was the drought in our soul. He will say, "When you felt so little, I felt so much. You overwhelmed My heart with that single glance of your eyes."

Mourning for the Bridegroom

"'Can the friends of the bridegroom mourn as long as the bridegroom is with them? But the days will come when the bridegroom will be taken away from them, and then they will fast'" (Matt. 9:15).

Jesus prophesied of this incessant longing that His friends would know when He no longer walked the earth. In essence, He said, "Oh, how they will miss Me in that day. Oh, how their hearts will mourn in My absence." This is the invitation He gives to His friends: an awakened heart full of love and an absent Beloved. It is the way of love that He has set for us. And, oh the pain of that invitation. How real is the pain of mourning. To love Him in this way of mourning is not mystical, nor theoretical, it is actual. We love a real Man, and He is not here with us as He was when He walked the earth. The gift He has given us in His absence is the friend of mourning and the pain of love's wound.

Lovesickness is wonderful in the sense that it exists and that it is for the Living God. Did we not pray that our hearts would break for Him? Did we not ask Him to cause our hearts to love Him? Yes, and He has surely come. And though we would not trade this wonderful mystery for anything, pain is pain is pain and, *oh, the pain* of wanting God when He does not come in the way that we desire Him to. Though lovesickness is about *love*, it nevertheless is a painful *sickness* that seizes the heart. Our longings clash into each other in an inward tantrum of desire. We have open hearts and one option for fulfillment. Our whole life is dependant and contingent on His coming to us. We mourn for Him. We fast in His absence. We cry out for His appearing. Though painful in nature, it is this sickness that in time escorts us into the very healing of our hearts.

How do we respond in these times when our heart bursts with longing and no answer comes forth from Heaven? First, we must seek to keep a right view of Jesus and to remember He is always after *greater love*. This keeps our hearts tender and not offended or unnecessarily wounded. It is so necessary to know the Divine motivation behind these seasons. He is not leaving us in the pains of love with any other incentive than love itself. He does not take pleasure in inflicting meaningless heartache upon us. Far from meaningless, these times are as Divine agents leading to greater love. They are instruments that make room for love to have its full way within our hearts. When we can connect the present pain to the future depth of love, our hearts are sustained for the duration. When we know that our current experience of heartache is in the ultimate Divine plan, we can embrace it as it was meant to be embraced and allow love to have its comprehensive way within us.

We must drink deeply of these invitations of lovesick desire. *Our* responsibility is to let longing have its way within us. These times are rare gifts, and we should seize them for their fullness rather than try to get by on as little as necessary. They are overflowing with invitations into greater love that are only awaiting our "yes." By the grace of God, and only by His grace, we must take every opportunity that these times present to us to grow in love. In this, we must remember that longing is a preparatory work that expands our souls. He will fill us according to our capacity to receive. We cannot enter into the fullness of love without these very essential enlargings of our hearts.

When the Bridegroom is away, we will mourn for Him (Matt. 9:15). Many times along our journey, we experience the absence of our Beloved's presence. Sometimes, this is through an actual season of Divine silence, and other times it is by the sheer paradox of a vision He gives our hearts for more of Him, which literally causes our present experience of Him to appear to us as utterly insufficient. One of the ways that our deep ache for God is exposed and increased is through fasting. Yet this kind of fast is very different than that which we have known. This mourning is a desperate longing for the joy and satisfaction of the Bridegroom. It is because we miss Him. We fast not to achieve God's attention but rather to enter into the very real gaze that we are already standing in. When Jesus spoke to John the Baptist's disciples about fasting, He spoke of it in terms of mourning for a Bridegroom. He said, *"When I am away, you will miss Me, and so you will fast."* He spoke of fasting as a way to enhance our experience of the full presence of the Bridegroom and the burning desires that are within His heart.

This realm of mourning is one of God's greatest secrets given to help us on the journey of the expanding of our hearts. It is as though He leans down from Heaven and whispers, "Friend, if you desire Me so, have sympathy for your little heart and add fasting to your prayers." God created such a mystery within the realm of fasting, and throughout all of history, believers have drank from the treasures therein. We will find our path to broaden beneath us with this simple heart-expander in place. Somehow, He designed that when we give ourselves voluntarily to this kind of weakness in order to make way for the experience of intimacy with our Lord, our hearts actually expand to receive more of Him. We touch what we cannot touch without the rawness and the weakness of the fastings. This fasting may be in the realm of food, time or giving. We fast our natural strength in fasting food, we fast our time by giving ourselves to prayer and we fast our

WE WILL FIND OUR PATH TO BROADEN BENEATH US WITH THIS SIMPLE HEART-EXPANDER IN PLACE.

financial strength by giving. Each are ways that we dive into voluntary weakness in order to desperately lean into the strength of our Beloved.

It has always been the case with lovers that when one is faint with love, food is far from thought. When the heart is sick with desire, the body and its natural needs silently surrender to their secondary position. Such is the case with this Bridegroom mourning. It is a fast motivated by desire and sustained by longing. The longing of our hearts arises to such a severe degree of intensity that we cannot eat or sleep until we find ourselves once more in the strength of His embrace. This is the kind of mourning Jesus described. He said, "Ah, when you have tasted of My love as a Bridegroom and then you suddenly cannot find Me, you will not fast out of duty but out of the heart wrenching desire of separated lovers."

It is true that there is a mourning that can only be awakened in separation. How can we mourn when He is with us face to face, pouring out His affections and love? The longing sleeps in those days. It stays resting within our hearts. For in the days that He is near, the longing is fulfilled. Yet take the Beloved away, even for just a moment, and the mourning has begun. It awakens with such a fierce fervency that we wonder at how we had not noticed it there before. Yes, when we feel Him near in His manifest presence, we are filled with love, but when He is away, we are *fierce* with love. We become as an awakened storm breaking with ardent desire. In that day, we give anything. We risk anything. We fear nothing. For the love of our Bridegroom, we are driven with torrents of affection and desire.

He is bringing forth a lovesick bride, voluntarily choosing Him in the face of every evil. The sleeping mourning must be awakened in the heart of the lover. We fast to remind our hearts that He has been taken away, for we have grown used to His absence. The fastings give way to mournings, and in mourning, we are invincible. No death can touch us, for all leads to Him. Nothing can hold us or bind us for we are already free. Our cry arises: "Bind my body, close my mouth, take away my name, and you have not conquered me. I am heartsick with love with eyes into another world. You cannot touch what has been wholly given to Him, for He has set His seal upon my heart and locked me away in freedom forever. My heart mourns a Bridegroom, and there is no mountain I would not climb, no sea I would not cross to be with Him, to meet His embrace."

In mourning, we are free. This lovesickness surrounds our hearts as a protective cloud in the hour of trouble. Thus we pray, "Awaken this mourning! Bring to rise this sleeping longing! Strengthen our fastings to increase our mournings. For the day has come when the Bridegroom has been taken. O fierce lovesick ones…O friends of the Bridegroom…Arise O mourning hearts!

"The Divine Wound of Longing"

All day my heart has ached. I have so longed to be with You. I have only known longing. Feelings. Emotions. Pain. Love. Desire. I love you, my sweet Beloved. I love you. I need you so. I am a fool lost in a sea of unnamed emotions, searching for a beacon, hoping that my True Love will take my thousand emotions and create a song of love for He Whom my heart loves.

If this pain is the sword of your love, I can think of no sweeter friend. If pain is my escort into deeper love, pain is my cherished companion. One of the most beautiful things about pain is that no matter the source, no matter the cause, it can always lead me to You and cause me to lean upon Your breast.

So an aching heart has been my reality all day. I know not why. If I were to hope, I would hope that this aching is your own drawing of my heart. I would hope that you were the Wounder of my heart today. You were the Piercer of my soul. You were the cause of my suffering. And truly it was only a taste. But if it was of You, than let me not only taste but drink, and drink deeply.

For as long as I can remember, I have wanted to want you. I have hungered to hunger. I have longed to long. If today You Yourself placed within my feeble heart but one drop of Divine longing, than I can think of no greater way to spend a day. A day of an aching heart…wounded by the One it aches for…made whole only in the Lover of its love.

I would gladly cry a thousand nights and drink of pain all of my days, if I could but know that the tears were kissed by the Divine before they became the fountain welling up within my Heart. If I could but know that the pain was birthed not in my own heart but in the Heart of the Man of Sorrows. If tears were not simply for the release of my own heart but for the sharing with You in Your sufferings, oh, the gold of those tears.

Draw me and I will run after You. This is my cry tonight, as I lay my tear-stained heart before You. I care not what tomorrow holds so long as You hold me tomorrow. So long as I know that You will meet in the morning with this same sweet closeness and even more. So long as I know that the night will not wash away the tenderness that fills my heart. So long as I know that You hold our love in the deep of Your heart and You guard it jealously with the Seal of all Seals. Amen.

"My One Desire"

To live in Love, my one desire.
To dwell in communion's internal fire.
To awaken in song and love in my dreams,
To dance my way into eternity.
You, O God, my breath within
Me the sail and You the wind.
Catch me away in gusty desire,
Consume my all in jealous fire.
Sweet Maker of my heart's design,
Hear my song and hear my cry.
Escort me into deeper realms,
Deep, deep places overwhelm.
Sweet and tender Love Divine,
Shepherd me to Your sweeter wine.
Let me find my way so sweet
Sinking before Your tear-stained feet,
Pouring my fragrance and all of my wealth,
Opening my heart to be filled with Thyself.
Tears and fragrance mingled as one.
This is my place and this is my song.
Find me here, in holy dance.
Keep me here, in Love's romance.
Do not stray, oh heart of mine,
But cling to love more sweet than wine.
Be your Beloved's in full not in part,
Always abiding in the love of His heart.
Yes, be your Beloved's and He be yours,
As you gracefully dance through Eternity's doors

CHAPTER 8

COMMUNION WITH THE BELOVED

"I sat down in His shade with great delight, and His fruit was so sweet to my taste.... Sustain me.... Refresh me...for I am lovesick" (Song Sol. 2:3-5).

And now that a chamber has been carved out within our hearts by the broad spade of longing, room has been made for God's greatest gift to the human heart: *Divine Love and communion with the Beloved*. Now remember, longing and dry desire are absolutely part of this gift. They are the reach of our hearts in drawing near to God and the promises of His coming. But now let us consider not only the promises but the *answers*. Let us reflect on when Jesus draws near to us in our experience. Let us look into what these preparatory gifts of hunger and thirst have been so pining after: communion with the Godhead.

The highest privilege God has given to the human race is the unthinkable invitation to enjoy intimacy with Himself. He keeps the angels within the boundary lines of servanthood, yet He gives invitation to the human race to enter into the unthinkable, in the realm of intimacy with Himself. The King has brought us into His chambers (Song Sol. 1:4). He invites us to cast ourselves into the depths of eternal love and fellowship with the Trinity. Yes, He delights to give Himself in holy intimacy to the hearts of men. Oh, great mystery of all time! That He would desire to exchange love with weak hearts such as ours! He glories in flooding earthen vessels with eternal treasure by pouring His own love into our hearts through His Holy Spirit. "…The love of God has been poured out into our hearts by the Holy Spirit who was given to us" (Rom. 5:5).

In this divine inflowing of love, God gives the human heart the greatest reward in this life and the life to come. He imparts His very love into our hearts (Jn. 17:26). He floods the dry beings of His friends with the river of His love by the Holy Spirit, and He tenderizes our hearts as we drink of this holy stream. This experience of premier delight breaks in upon our hearts with supernatural softening. Not only do we *receive* His love, but we experience the sheer joy of loving Him in return. Do we not love to *feel* our own hearts moving in love for Him? He reaches into the chambers within us where the swelling river of His love abides, and He draws it back to Himself with all of our desires and affections for Him swallowed within its flowing return. We find ourselves rich with love for our Beloved. "We love Him because He first loved us" (1 Jn. 4:19). Our hearts overflow with the magnificent theme of His beauty, and we abound with love songs unto Him (Ps. 45:1). The glory of our existence is in this divine exchange. *The reward of our lives now and for all eternity is to love Him and to receive His love.*

Lovesick Communion

The maiden expresses this treasure in Song of Solomon. In the resting beneath His shade, she finds the utter sweetness of His fruit to her taste (Song Sol. 2:3). Her heart responds, "Your love is most sweet! I delight to rest in Your embrace." She has finally found the secret to a satisfied life. No longer grasping after the wind for things that do not remain and no longer striving in works to gain His approval, she sinks down into the warmth of *eternal* pleasure to receive the free gift of Love offered to her. Her heart has truly moved into the enjoyment of His affections. She loves feeling beautiful and desired by Him. She delights in the revelation of His beauty to her.

She describes herself as *sick with love* for her Beloved (2:5). Out of the overflow of His affections for her, she discovers her own heart's response in genuine enjoyment and pleasure. It is so much and so rich there is no other description than sickness. Oh, but a holy sickness it is! It is a sickness that, in fact, denotes a certain health of soul—for she has finally found all of her fountains within Him, and it is in the very tasting of this spiritual milk that empowers her to flee ungodliness (1 Pet. 2:3). Her desires are no longer motionless when she beholds the Lord but rather a whirlwind of intoxication. She is captivated by who He is. She has been wounded by the arrow of His love and finds her only consolation in the greater tasting of it—each taste making her more lovesick than before. She cries out, "Sustain me...refresh me... for I am lovesick!" (Song Sol. 2:5).

There is nothing more thrilling to our souls than when God reveals Himself to us. Our spirits were created to pine away with longing for God and to not be consoled except in more revelation of Him. More of God is the only answer to longing's ache, and yet what we soon find is that as one longing is satisfied with a new revelation of Him, an even larger yearning takes its place. As He enlarges our capacity and then fills that space with more of Himself, a greater desire than we had known previously is awakened within. We find that only in the greater tasting are we sustained, and only in more of Him are we refreshed.

To see more of Him is to desire more of Him, and to desire more of Him is to eventually see more of Him, for He satisfies those who hunger and thirst for Him, and He fills the hungry with good things (Ps. 107:9). Expectant eyes look to Him and He gives them their food in due season, opening His hand and satisfying their desire (Ps. 145:15, 16). So on and on, we scale the endless ascent of God's love. It is both pain and comfort, hunger and satisfaction, desire and fulfillment. An eternal occupation of asking and receiving, of hungering and being satisfied. We will forever gaze upon His beauty, long for the greater unfolding of His glory, be overcome by the revelation that He gives and then cry out for more of Him once again with even greater ardency and desperation.

COMMUNION WITH GOD IS THE CONTINUAL EXPRESSION AND EXPERIENCE OF MUTUAL AFFECTION BETWEEN GOD AND THE HUMAN HEART.

Understanding Communion

"As the Father has loved Me, I also have loved you; abide in My love.... These things I have spoken to you, that My joy may remain in you, and that your joy may be full"
(Jn. 15:9-11).

To abide in love is to commune continually with the One we adore. Jesus invites each heart into this residing in divine affection with one of the most compelling confessions of His love ever communicated. He begins with expressing the worth of the love in which He invites us to abide within. This love that Jesus possesses for me and beckons me to continually immerse my heart in is only to be compared to the love that the Father possesses for *Him*. It is the same love. The way that the Father feels for the Son is the way that the Son feels for me!!! Unfathomable reward of the ages! It is in context to this description of His love that He beckons the heart, saying, "Stay here in My love, and do not depart from its embrace! Abide with Me in this love divine, and you shall know fullness of joy."

Love is not love until it is expressed. Communion with God is the continual expression and experience of mutual affection between God and the human heart. It is the embrace of Jesus Christ and the kiss of His Word upon our hearts (Song Sol. 1:2). Communion is the exchange of love, with or without words. It is the presence of love that leads to greater presence and the fulfillment of desire that breaks open greater desire. Ah, the beauty of His nearness! The One who is fairer than all the sons of men with grace poured richly upon His lips—He is the one that pours the warm and fragrant oil of gladness into the deep of our hearts (Ps. 45:2, 7)!! Our every fountain is enveloped in His River of Pleasures, and our every consolation encompassed within Himself. He is the supreme delight of the ages. He is the glorious sweetness of all eternity. This is our Beloved. This is our Friend!

Surely anyone who has tasted of His goodness will give testimony to the ruining nature of its uniqueness. We are forever ruined for anything less and forever caught up in holy pursuit of more of Him when we have but tasted a morsel of His magnificence. David expressed invitation to the saints, "Oh, taste and see that the Lord is good; blessed is the man who trusts in Him! Oh, fear the Lord, you His saints! There is no want to those who fear Him" (Ps. 34:8-9). To describe the beauty and the wonder of this Beloved God, the psalmist declares, "I have seen the consummation of all perfection..." (Ps. 119:96). With the heart of one possessed and owned by love, Paul declared, "Yet indeed I also count all things loss for the excellence of the knowledge of Christ Jesus my Lord..." (Phil. 3:8). And Mary of Bethany spoke not with words but with action, pouring out her life inheritance over Jesus in one act of extravagant adoration. The fragrance that arose from that room forever and ever gives testimony to the beauty and the worth of the Man Christ Jesus (Mk. 14). If her devotion came with words she might have said, "Before me is the One who is worthy of the love of all creation, and God has graced me with one moment in time to ascribe to Him His worth."

Our Desire for Communion

Every human being has within his soul this reach. And as we move deeper in the realm of intimacy, we have no option but to desire more and more of the eternal pleasure of knowing Him. We find that we cannot live unless we know and experience greater correspondence between God and our own soul. We long to be His friends and to share the secrets of His heart. We have known the ache of our own longing, but just as love is not love without this longing, love is not love without satisfaction. We must *experience* that which we have waited for. The feast of communion is our desire. For surely His love is better than wine (Song Sol. 1:2). It is better than the finest things of life, and our entire reward is wrapped up within it. When we have tasted of the drink found within the River of Pleasures, we are abundantly satisfied with God's fullness (Ps. 36:8). It is this that we are after, and it is for this that He has made us to receive.

We were made to know more than longing. We were made to taste. He designed us not just as those who would grow in capacity of hunger, becoming spacious hearts of desire. He has made us to receive and to experience love Himself. This is our glory. This is our crown. We were made for the fullness of joy. "'These things I have spoken to you, that My joy may remain in you, and that your joy may be full'" (Jn. 15:11). We were made to fully enjoy our Beloved Jesus, to the fullness of our capacity. Communion with God therefore is more than the desire for Him; it is the enjoyment of Him. It is the present tense fellowship of superior delight.

We desire real experience in real time. We were designed by our Creator to crave His nearness and to only be satisfied in the true experience of love within us. For this reason, it is not wrong that we so cry out for His presence. It is not too much to ask that we might know Him as richly as we would dare dream about. Oh, how much greater are His own dreams for our hearts. God dreamed a dream of me in my creation, and that dream is larger than any lofty vision I have ever conceived of. Much has been said about the faithfulness of God to bring us into our purpose or our destiny. Yet the destiny God is most determined to answer is His purpose for each heart to know communion with His Son. He Himself will be faithful to bring each one into that place of divine love that He has purposed for their heart. "God is faithful, by whom you were called into the fellowship of His Son, Jesus Christ our Lord" (1 Cor. 1:9).

COMMUNION WITH GOD... IS MORE THAN THE DESIRE FOR HIM; IT IS THE ENJOYMENT OF HIM.

God's Nearness in Communion

Communion with God is the place from which we were brought forth and the place to which we will return, for surely we were made to commune with the living God and to desire such. It is not presumptuous but befitting to our rightful understanding of our spiritual inheritance. When we aspire to be so transformed that we might dwell with these everlasting burnings (Is. 33:14), we are aspiring rightly. For there we were designed to abide. Even from the garden,

God's invitation was for man to live in unhindered love, with all of the heart, soul, mind and strength. We were made to live in perpetual communion with our loving God. And from this intrinsic part of our very design, we have longed and desired for this very constant communication and relations with our God.

Though it feels so far from our understandings, God describes this place of Love's richness as not too mysterious and not too far off. It is not so high in heaven that we cannot reach it. Nor is it beyond the sea that we cannot grasp it. It is near. It is in our mouths and in our hearts (Deut. 30:11-14). God spoke these words to resist the lies that would come against His covenant of wholehearted love. For surely something within us thinks this communion with God unattainable. "God does not reveal Himself to me in that way," we say with despairing voices. We write ourselves off by thinking it is for another and not for our own hearts. Yet how far from true is this conclusion. Our God desires that each one not only be filled with longing for Him, but indeed find the experiential consolations of His nearness that longing has so faithfully prepared us for.

We treat this realm of the experience of Love as though it were indeed "so far off." Even in our cries of longing, we give evidence of how mysterious we think it is. "Oh God, why are You so far? When will You come near?" We continually speak to Him as though He is in the habit of bounding from one location to another instead of what is true, that His omnipresence swallows up all locations. There is no height so high that He is not above and no depth so low that He is not beneath it. When we feel that He is far from us, before we rush to conclusions that He is disciplining or ignoring us, let us first ask if He is in fact near and we simply do not know it. "'Surely the Lord is in this place, and I did not know it'" (Gen. 28:16).

He is near to us. He is the high and lofty One, yet He dwells with the contrite in spirit (Is. 57:15). This causes me to consider, if God be so near, surely I must know Him more than I think I know Him. And surely I must hardly know Him at all. If God be so near, He is near before I am aware. And if God be so near then how far is my heart from knowing Him in His nearness? Still, God is near to me. If I feel that I do know Him in His nearness, than my mind is last to touch this know-ing. Perhaps, my spirit knows Him deeply for He dwells within its chambers. Closer than my brother, friend or spouse, He dwells within me. He could not be nearer. Yet still this mystery seems just out of reach. As if part of me is knowing some-thing that another part has not yet comprehended. It is beyond, beyond, so far beyond my understanding. And my understanding may very well be the last to partake of such glory that I speak of. For love indeed surpasses knowledge, and where the mind is limited, love is inexhaustible. Even so, I was made to know the God who has come near, and I was made to experience Him in His nearness.

I WAS MADE TO KNOW THE GOD WHO HAS COME NEAR, AND I WAS MADE TO EXPERIENCE HIM IN HIS NEARNESS.

And thus, from our hearts comes forth this cry: "O God, if it is truly so present in Your heart to be near, then cause me to experience the nearness I am already standing in. Let me not call times of refreshing times of silence because of my unbelief in Your coming. Let me not possess a mindset that believes this dryness and emptiness to be acceptable, getting used to my lack of experience under the premise that You do not desire to come. Rather, let me know the true nature of Your heart, the desire that You possess to be near to those You love."

Much of our longing and aching does not come out of an accurate understanding of God's true proximity to us. He is near when we imagine Him far. We call times of refreshing times of silence not because He is actually silent but because of our unbelief in His nearness, or simply because of our unlikeness to Him, and thus our inability to recognize Him. This is not to negate true times of silence or true winter seasons where He is very purposefully hiding Himself for the furtherance of love (as exemplified by the bride in Song of Solomon chapter five). Yet many times we think we are in winter when in fact we are in spring. Again, the reason for this is both our doubt that He ever manifests His nearness to us in our experience and also our lack of knowledge of His heart. He is in our world, and our world does not recognize Him.

We must be careful to not possess a mentality that spiritual barrenness is what is normal or a belief that this emptiness we are experiencing is simply the way God desires it. The idea that the common way to live in this age is to move blindly in the dark because He has not chosen to reveal Himself is a false mindset. Instead, we must know this about our God: He has come near out of His great desire, and He is jealous that we would experience His nearness and His presence. He is not a God who takes pleasure in being far off. He is the only God that has delighted to not only come near, but to become one of us in order to bring us to Himself. "For it the God who commanded light to shine out of darkness, who has shone in our hearts to give the light of the knowledge of the glory of God in the face of Jesus Christ" (2 Cor. 4:6).

His Desire for Communion

He desires that we experience Him. To know Him intimately and closely is not something only I desire. Once again, I desire His presence because He desires to be present to me. I long to find Him in His nearness because He longs to be found by me. "And you will seek Me and find Me, when you search for Me with all of your heart. I will be found by you, says the Lord..." (Jer. 29:13-14). Surely, this is our confidence as we cry out for this depth of communion. To find a person that desires God's nearness is not a rare discovery. For, in fact, every person on the earth has this desire though it may not be identified as such. Yet a God that desires to be found by His people, this is the rarity. And it is more than a rarity. It is beyond belief. Who is like Him among the gods? (Ps. 86:8).

A god that would desire to bring his subjects near is nonexistent except for in one single instance. It is only found once in all of heaven and earth and for all eternity. And it is found in the heart of our God. "For since the beginning of the world men have not heard nor perceived by the ear, nor has the eye seen any God besides You, who acts for the one who waits for Him. You meet him who rejoices and does righteousness, who remembers You in Your ways" (Is. 64:4-5). And not only is He the only One who has brought His subjects near; He is the only One who (oh, unfathomable gift) has called His subjects friends and desired relationship with them to be in the glorious realm of intimacy!!

This desire founded in God's heart was made most manifest by the coming of the only Begotten of the Father and is forever continually guaranteed by the beloved Spirit Indwelling. Nothing is greater evidence of God's desire to be near mankind than the Incarnation of the Beloved Son. "For God so loved the world that He gave His only begotten Son" (Jn. 3:16). For all eternity this stands as the great witness of God's purpose of nearness to human beings. Within His blood, Jesus has forever eliminated the place of distance between God and man. "But now in Christ you who once were far off have been brought near by the blood of Christ" (Eph. 2:13).

And as we walk this age of time, this small window being swallowed up in eternity's enclosing, the Father has given us of the Holy Spirit who is the great Comforter of our souls. This also is the unutterable, irrefutable argument towards God's desire for nearness. He gave us of His Holy Spirit. And this Person of the Holy Ghost could not be any nearer to us. He dwells within our very beings!! We, as individual souls, are the temples in which He abides not only in this age, but forever and ever. "'And I will ask the Father, and he will give you another Counselor to be with you forever—the Spirit of truth. The world cannot accept him, because it neither sees him nor knows him. But you know him, for he lives with you and will be in you" (Jn. 14:16-17, NIV).

Communion with the Indwelling Spirit

"The grace of the Lord Jesus Christ, and the love of God, and the communion of the Holy Spirit be with you all" (2 Cor. 13:14).

In some of their last hours together, the Beloved Jesus told His disciples that He was departing from them and going away. After He spoke this, He imparted comfort to their hearts with the words, "...I tell you the truth. It is to your advantage that I go away; for if I do not go away, the Helper will not come to you; but if I depart, I will send Him to you" (Jn. 16:7). With these words, Jesus opened one of the most astonishing windows of revelation about the glory of the New Covenant. Jesus said in essence, "Friends, you have known My presence on the earth. You have walked with Me, talked with Me, known me in laughter and sorrow. You truly are My friends. Yet I tell you the truth; there is a mystery in the eternal plan of the Godhead that transcends the intimacy we have yet known. In My leaving, I will send you a gift that will far outweigh the enjoyment you would experience if I were to stay here. The mystery is this: I will dwell inside of you through the Holy Spirit." With these words, Jesus described the place where the words of life that He had spoken to his friends would actually become written on their hearts and minds through the Holy Spirit (Heb. 8:10).

Our God has come nearer to us than any man or angel would have thought conceivable. Within our very spirit, the third Person of the Trinity dwells. We stand before a God who has given Himself to dwell within the hearts of men. He has put His Spirit within our very beings, causing us to be temples of the living God. Surely, a vast world resides within every believer called *the God of love*. "'...The kingdom of God is within you'" (Lk. 17:21). The God who is Love abides within us through His Spirit (1 Jn. 4:16). He has given us something and Someone far beyond our understandings in this Gift of all time. He has sent to us a very real Person—as God as the Father is God—that we might know communion with God Himself. We need not search for Him as for a fleeting shadow we are trying to grasp. Rather, we may always find Him as the indwelling Friend so present and so near.

He, who proceeds from the Father (Jn. 15:26) as the glorious gift of God (Jn. 4:10), is an ocean of divine love, a flowing River, a continual movement of Love within, an abiding stream indwelling, a supernatural current of affection. He is the One that God has sent to pour out the Love of the Godhead into our hearts (Rom. 5:5). In Him, we know communion with the Be-

> *IN HIM, WE KNOW COMMUNION WITH THE BELOVED.*

loved. He is the One who searches the deep things of God, and His premiere responsibility is to reveal the Person of Jesus to our hearts. His sole purpose is to bring us into greater intimacy and greater love with the Son of God and, oh, how He loves His job description!

Oh, how He delights to bring the sons of God into the true knowledge of Jesus Christ.

We experience intimacy with God through communion with the Holy Spirit. He is the fountain that Jesus said would spring up into everlasting life to whoever drinks of it (Jn. 4:14). He is the rivers of living water that will flow from our hearts as we believe in Him in the way the scripture describes (Jn. 7:37). His work is to glorify Jesus to us by revealing His heart and imparting knowledge inside of us. He has come to utterly immerse us in the love of God, leaving no part of our hearts not saturated with the fullness of His sweetness. The mystery of God is about this fiery Lover, the Holy Spirit, consuming redeemed human beings and bringing them into union with God.

Above all else, this is our primary calling in life: *to live lives immersed in God.* And it is the Holy Spirit that accomplishes this work within us. God unites us to Himself by dwelling in the very midst of our beings and uniting us to Himself. Our God has allowed that we could pass from death into life by passing into Him. When we enter into this immersion, it is the ultimate artwork of God on the earth. It is the union of God and man. The angelic hosts can only peer from a distance into this mystery that God has invited lovers of God into.

WE EXPERIENCE INTIMACY WITH GOD THROUGH COMMUNION WITH THE HOLY SPIRIT.

This living Being, the indwelling Christ, has come to abide within us that we might drink of intimacy with the Trinity in Love *unto the glorious transforma-*

136

tion of our souls. "But we all, with unveiled face, beholding as in a mirror the glory of the Lord, are being transformed into the same image form glory to glory, just as by the Spirit of the Lord" (2 Cor. 3:18). It is through the beholding of God, the Holy Spirit, that we are transformed from glory to glory.

We receive His transforming love in prayer through the release of the Divine Embrace of the Holy Spirit in the inner man. Love is infused into us by His Spirit in this place of communion, and it is here that we get lost in the immersion of Divine Love. It is here that we are ruined forever in lovesick adoration. When He— through the intoxicating immersion of the Holy Spirit— infuses us with Divine Love, we become as those of another world. We reach "the point of no return" not by willpower but by unyielding affection and continuous delight. Again, this is our primary calling. From this Divine Immersion flows everything else. We love from this place; we serve from this place; we live from this place.

Communion without Language

The road to this immersion begins with my filling my mind with the Word of God that the Holy Spirit might ignite it as fire in my inner man. Spirit must marry with Truth inside of me. The warmth of this tenderizing causes the truths of God to become alive within me and enkindles my heart for wholehearted obedience. When my mind is aligned with truth and I lovingly bring that truth before Him, the Holy Spirit touches that truth with fire, and the Word and the Spirit kiss on the inside of me. The Word of God is alive. It is a living flame. It is a furnace of supernatural substance that lives outside of time and space and yet inside of time and space as well. It is the eternal brought into time. And the way that it comes alive in fire within me is through the union of itself with the indwelling Spirit. In this, is true worship (Jn. 4:23-24). In this, is communion. As we keep His word by letting it abide in us continually, the love of God is perfected within us (1 Jn. 1:5). As we dwell in this place of communion with God, He is writing His name upon our minds and hearts (Jer. 31:33-34). He is kindling living flames in the hearts of His friends.

In this keeping of His Word, we soon find that it is more than ideas found in teachings, sermons or study. It is about ideas and truths we know of God entering into the hidden recesses of the inner man. They explode when they touch the spirit. This is the might of God exploding on the inside of the weak human frame (Eph. 3:16). They begin as words and end as burning realities. They start as concepts but become *experiences* in God. They expand within us and stretch their boundaries far beyond the natural confinement of time and space. They are without limit, for they are living truths of love that eternally remain. They begin as words, for syllables and concepts are the package surrounding very real realities. Yet when these fiery realities wrapped in words are accepted into the chamber of our beings, they find

> *IT IS MORE THAN IDEAS FOUND IN TEACHINGS, SERMONS OR STUDY. IT IS ABOUT IDEAS AND TRUTHS WE KNOW OF GOD ENTERING INTO THE HIDDEN RECESSES OF THE INNER MAN.*

their rightful vessel, and in time, the titles that once held them are cast aside and no longer needed. The living substance now abides within the human heart. The reality of "God is Love" is eternal, yet the words and syllables come only as a temporary service to tote the reality around until it finds its home within the secret place of the human heart.

I imagine the Holy Spirit, the Wind of God, catching up these words and concepts into His wings and rushing them into the center of my being. There He breathes upon them, and as I ponder them, mulling over them with much love and meditation, they eventually ignite into a living flame. At this point, there is no longer need for words or concepts. They have already done their duty. Language is left behind

> *LANGUAGE IS LEFT BEHIND SMILING, FOR SHE HAS ACCOMPLISHED HER GOD-ORDAINED RESPONSIBILITY, AND NOW THE FLAME BURNS ON ITS OWN.*

smiling, for she has accomplished her God-ordained responsibility, and now the flame burns on its own. She remains within the boundaries of what can be communicated while the burning reality that once required ideas and concepts to be understood now takes me upon its wings into the realm of love far surpassing knowledge and ascends eternally into the great Beyond.

Communing Prayer

"...I bow my knees to the Father...that He would grant you, according to the riches of His glory, to be strengthened with might through His Spirit in the inner man, that Christ may dwell in your hearts through faith; that you, being rooted and

grounded in love, may be able to comprehend with all the saints what is the width and length and depth and height—to know the love of Christ which passes knowledge; that you may be filled with the fullness of God" (Eph. 3:14–19).

And now before closing this everlasting subject, we must look briefly at how we move into this exchange of love from day to day. We do this simply through waiting before Him in prayerful love. We position ourselves for communion with Jesus by coming before Him day after day in devotional prayer. We bring our cold hearts before the fire of His love, and we sit before Him as Mary did, with a heart of gazing adoration. We gaze upon the Spirit indwelling with the eyes of our heart, speaking gentle words of love and thanksgiving and posturing our hearts to receive His own affection for us. Sometimes, we wait in silence, gently receiving His love. Our part is to come before Him in love and to gaze upon the Beloved Friend Indwelling. His part is to ignite our beings with love through the supernatural impartation of Divine Love within us.

And this Divine igniting is what the Beloved Spirit of God is committed to. Oh, how He desires to bring forth fiery lovers of Jesus from the human race. When we come before Him and wait in love and worship, He causes love to abound within us. He strengthens our inner man with the might of Divine Love, causing us to know in our experience how high and how wide, how deep and how long is the love of Christ. He is bringing us increasingly into the fullness of God. And this is His delight. O Blessed Third Person of the Trinity! How we love Your jealousy over our little hearts! Take us, we pray, into Divine Love's fullness, leaving us not at introductions but ever moving into transformation and fullness! Prepare us in adorned and purified love for our Beloved Jesus!!

OH, JESUS! How we desire communion with You! How we love Your every unfolding and Your every kiss upon our hearts! The incomparable pleasures of Your love have made saints throughout history to walk in the incurable lovesickness of divine delight. We have tasted and we have seen that You are good! You have ruined us forever for anything inferior to Your heavenly embrace. We want only to abide in Your love, absorbed forever in Your great affections. For truly Your love is better than wine and better than life. It is our reward, our life, our breath, and our all!!

Oh, how He has loved us by this exchange! Oh, how He has won our hearts by this fellowship! And, oh, how this communion prepares us for all of the many days when His manifest presence is so seemingly absent from our experience. How it anchors us in the seasons when we have only faith in a God unseen and hope for an answer yet to come.

"Hidden with Christ"

I have died. As has been my prayer, dear Lord, help me to truly die. Only the dead are free—free, faceless, unknown beings that hide themselves in Him. If they are seen, and only by true lovers of God can it be so, they are seen only in the shadows, in one fleeting flash and then it is gone. The dead. They are the free. Unbound by a word—whether it be praise or insult. No longer made by physical essence that can be wounded or held down and caged. They fly on wings of freedom and soar above the things of earth.

Hidden with Christ in God. Only You truly see me. Only You know who I truly am and the treasure that is hidden deep. Only You can hear the song of my heart, for it also is hidden in You. And one glorious Day, when by God, You are revealed, when You my Life, my Breath, my Song, indeed my very Heart, are revealed...on that day then I too will be revealed with You in glory. But now I am hidden. I live among the dead. And there I am free from the things of earth and of this passing life. Only Your eyes see me. Only You behold me in truth. I am hidden with You in God.

CHAPTER 9

BELIEVING IN THE UNSEEN

We have joined ourselves to an Ocean, and we cleave to a world unseen. It is not only a *joining* that we embrace but a *free-falling*. Yes, I join myself to this Ocean, but what is more, I free-fall with arms spread wide into its engulfing. And in my descent, a drawn out cry comes forth as my last request, *"Have Your way!"* Into His hands, I commit my spirit (Ps. 31:5). I have died, and I no longer live. I have no more rights. Swallowed up in the great deep of my transcendent God, fully His forever. I have taken His name, and my entire identity has been absorbed by Himself. I know not where these waves will take me...yet always to a deeper deep and a greater love. I freefall with arms spread wide, holding nothing for myself and keeping not the slightest grip of ownership upon my life. My life is not my own. I have been bought with a price. And I have willingly surrendered to my position of hiddenness in Him—hidden with Christ in God. When He appears, I too will appear with Him (Col 3:4).

Dangling in the Unseen

When we leave the places of living before men and begin to live before the Eyes-of-fire alone, we cross over into unknown territory. As we looked at in the process of His awakening, He has brought us to a certain wilderness of transformation. And here in this place we are no longer able to measure our worth by the tangible reality of our success before men. We leave the old measuring sticks at the door, for they are not suited for the ways of God. We depart from the false identity that was based on how respected, known, gifted and influential we were in the eyes of men and leap into the vast unknown realm, the hidden reality, of who we are eternally in God. In this hurdle, we take great risk for we leave every familiar comfort behind us. To abandon the realm of the seen that we might freefall into the unseen is a daring endeavor and only faith anchors our souls. We voluntarily jump off the cliff of our old identity without an absolute clarity of our new one. Though we know who we are in the corporate sense of the redeemed-body-of-Christ, the mysteries that He formed in us individually and the details of who we are personally in the hidden places, are nearly entirely hidden from our understandings.

We are trading in what we have always known and what others have always told us of ourselves for a book of blank pages. We leave all the old voices, however true or false, for the One voice who is temporarily very silent in our experience. He shows us so little of who we are in Him in the beginning because He wants us to experience the "drop off" from the old ways and be willing to plunge into the unseen realm with eyes of faith. We face the pain of the barrenness of our souls. We face the reality of all that we do not yet know of Him when we once thought we knew so much. We spend a season in this dangling-in-between place—no longer identified as we once were, yet still so foreign and distant from who we truly are in Him and our eternal identity. As we dangle, we pray, "Let me be weighed on honest scales, that God may know my integrity" (Job 31:6).

In this season of "dangling," we slowly and nearly imperceptibly experience a transfer of all of our wealth. Our "gold" and all that we are are moved from what is seen into the hidden realm of the unseen. "Then you will lay your gold in the dust....Yes, the Almighty will be your gold and your precious silver; for then you will have your delight in the Almighty..." (Job 22:24-25). What we cling to is no longer of the essence of what is temporal but what is eternal. We are hidden with Christ until He is revealed and us with Him. We leave the realm of what can be communicated and stake our territory in the temporary silence of eternal reality.

IN THIS PLACE, THE COST IS THE SILENCE. THE PRICE IS THE HIDDENNESS.

In this place, the cost is the silence. The price is the hiddenness. No one, except those rare few with eyes into eternity can perceive who we are anymore. We cannot communicate except by such feeble words that never do justice to the beauty or the wonder of what He Himself calls us in Him. The pain is the namelessness. Though we are far from nameless in truth, we simply have not heard the very real name He has given to us and that we will possess for all eternity. This is the cost and, oh, how worth it is the sacrifice. It is this struggle that brings forth strength within us in time. We place all of our riches and all of our inheritance in the realm beyond. We wish we could reach it, but we cannot. It is hidden. It is behind a veil. Yet it *is* there. And we begin to know by the testimony of the Spirit within us that we own a very real and genuine *reality* in that place outside of the seen.

Unseen Transformation

In this place of hiddenness, as we surrender to the Hand that has led us to this wilderness, great transformation is happening within our souls. And it is for this transformation into His likeness that He has brought us here. We are changed by Love in this place. He has us on a journey unto communion and unto fullness, and as we give ourselves to Him wholeheartedly, we are transformed into becoming more and more like Him. Christ is progressively formed in us (Gal. 4:19). As we become more like Him, taking on His likeness, so also we increase in our experience of His nearness.

This gives language to one of the very significant reasons that we so often do not experience the feeling of His presence in this wilderness place. One of the contributors to this real delay is the simple element of our own unlikeness to Him. When we do not experience the presence of God, when our prayers for God's nearness seem to be answered only by silence, much of the distance we feel is purely that we have not yet grown like Him enough to recognize Him. He is near yet we are unable to experience His nearness.

Yet this is no cause for alarm. Again, this dilemma is precisely why we are here, and He has us right where He desires us. He is going to so change us into His likeness. And in that transformation, we will no longer be hindered in experiencing the nearness of God that we are already standing in. He has great jealousy to bring us to the place where we *do* experience Him and hear His voice. He is deeply transforming us so that we might know the fullness of His love and the vast regions of who He is. As our inner man is transformed so also our intimacy with God will deepen. Yet this transformation is indeed a process and a journey. He has much to teach us not only in the experience of divine presence and the hearing of God's voice but in the encounter of divine delays and the silence of God. It is in the confrontation of God's silence that we most submit to the unseen part of the transformation.

> *HE IS TURNING OUR LOFTY WORDS INTO DEEP REALITIES.*

The Unseen Work of God's Silence

We cry out for His coming, for His presence. In His delay, we are pained. With great fervor and ardency, we lift our voice, our heart and our desires in holy petitions. We find greater heartache than that which initially drove us to this place of desperation. He is testing our desire with the refining fire. He is turning our *lofty words* into *deep realities*. Under the hand of this testing, our groans grow weak. Tears are prevalent for we do not know what He is after, and our natural minds cannot understand this process of love.

In these times, He keeps our hearts alive by secretly blowing upon our hearts, causing our faint cries to become a bit stronger. At this renewal, we lift up our voice once more with fresh hope of His coming. Once more we find silence. Over and over, again and again, we move through these highs and lows of hunger's pathway. Times of hoping, times of fainting, and all are necessary. Though we cannot discern Him, He is personally attending to the fruition of our love by gently guiding us along and carefully nurturing our hearts like tender plants of desire.

He starves out our hunger and refines our desire while at the same time secretly sustaining our hope and strength to uphold us in the way. In this process, He creates a heart with one lifeline. He makes Himself the one Love and one Fear of our hearts by starving us out for Him alone. He readies us for His presence and prepares the way of His coming by this unavoidable wilderness way. In His apparent absence, the pain we experience chisels away our false motivations and makes right our wrong places. It causes what is unimportant to be seen in its true insignificance and what is essential to be received as such. He stretches our small capacities far beyond what we would have thought possible. He prepares the way for His coming by the very process of the journey's waiting and the pain of His delays. We begin to lean. If we *needed* Him before, we *cling* to Him now. Nothing and no one to return to. We sold everything to have Him and will never again find satisfaction in any secondary consolation.

In these times, He asks us to *remember Him in love* even when all circumstances seem to sing a different song. It is a question asked by the silence itself. If it were to come with audible words and discernable presence, we would answer much more readily. Yet the great Lover knows that His questions are not to be answered with haste, and our answers must be accompanied with faith. We look into the dark cloud of unknowing and see with the eyes of faith the heart of our Beloved.

We must learn to face our own emerging questions. We question His distance. We wonder at His reasons for not coming to us in His presence. His ways are mysterious to us, and every accusation would seek to convince us of falsities about His heart. We are forced to ask ourselves: "Will I rise above any doubts of His character and His love for me and answer a question that I have not actually heard with my ears but only with the memory of what I have known of Him? Will I now do what I promised Him and remember that all His ways with me are love and this silence also, though dismal in its hollowness, is truly rich with all of love's hidden movements? "We will remember your love" (Song Sol. 1:4).

> *WE QUESTION HIS DISTANCE. WE WONDER AT HIS REASONS FOR NOT COMING TO US IN HIS PRESENCE.*

Our "yes's" to Him must own a history by the end of their journey. It is a "yes" that we will say so many times along the journey, and a thousand choices will be included in its final testimony. We say, "Yes," to He whom we cannot see, answering a question our natural ears have not actually heard. With faith, we interpret His silence as an invitation to give Him our love. We choose to believe that all His ways are love, therefore knowing that His silence is not His refusal of our requests but the very workings of Love Himself in our hearts. With the hidden help of the Holy Spirit's wooing, we arise while it is yet night in our soul and say, *"Yes. To all that You are. To all of Your ways. I believe in Your love. I will have no other loves but You. I believe that even Your silence is Your love for me and I say, 'Yes,' to Your hand upon my heart. Have Your way within my heart and take me to the fullness of love."*

The Unseen Fellowship of God's Silence

In Song of Solomon 5, Jesus appears to the maiden in the garments of Gethsemane. His head is covered with the dew of the night. He asks her the question that He asked His sleep-hungry disciples on His lonesome night in the garden—"Will you watch with Me? Will you endure this night with me and fellowship with me even in its blackness?" When the maiden arises to go with Him, she finds Him gone. The silence begins. This time His silence is not rooted in the immaturity of her unlikeness to Him. Rather, He is withholding His presence to yet refine and deepen her mature love for Him. He has given her invitation to suffer with Him, but the critical part of that suffering is His very absence. The Lamb's greatest suffering was His Father's silence on the cross. It was not the beating, the torment from the people nor even the rejection from His friends. It was His Father's absence that caused His heart to burst with sorrow.

Because of the cross and redemption, we are never again separated from His love. We will never know what Jesus knew on the cross. Never will we find Him turned from us. Never will He reject us. Yet He does take us through seasons where He withholds His manifest presence from us in order to bring forth even greater and stronger love from our hearts. He refines our love by the fire of His felt absence. There are two sides of love: the dance and the dirge. One cannot know Love's fullness without the drinking of both cups. He takes from us the experience of His nearness, and in its place, we find the strike and the woundings of the watchmen. We encounter the pain of others around us saying, "Where is He now? Why don't you call on Him if He is so real?"

This is the heart's greatest test—a twofold test—the absence of our Beloved and the presence of every kind of torment and suffering. Every voice around us and every circumstance upon us declare His abandonment of us. And all we hear from Heaven is the sound of stillness. The Lamb waits. He waits for our voice to arise. This question asked by His silence must be voiced for His Father asked it of Him, and it is only in this complexity of pres-sure that we will ultimately drink the cup of the fellowship of sufferings. He awaits our voice to rise from the pain of the struggle and say, "I love Him! I commit my spirit into His hands! I am His! I believe in His love. He will not abandon me forever. Soon His voice will break

HE REFINES OUR LOVE BY THE FIRE OF HIS FELT ABSENCE. THERE ARE TWO SIDES OF LOVE: THE DANCE AND THE DIRGE.

into this dark night, and He will vindicate Me with His presence once again."

For this cry of faith and love the Lamb waits. He holds back the thunder of heaven and the legions of angels in anticipation of what a small heart on the earth will voluntarily choose in the way of love. He says to the powers that wait for His bidding, "Do not answer her yet. We must wait. Angels be still. Promises, hold your place in the unanswered-residences. Hope, remain in the unseen; for hope that is seen is not hope. Dawning of the day, keep back your bright rays for but a few more moments. My beloved one is about to speak. She is about to choose Me in the darkest night. The words she will say will be recorded and remembered for all our eternity together. Thousands upon thousands of times in the ages to come I will remind her of these choices she is about to make. We must wait. We must make room for the heart of the volunteer to come forth. It is My way. She *will* volunteer her love freely" (Ps. 110:3).

From this place of darkness and silence, we lift our voice. Though we cannot see Him nor feel Him and though our surroundings seek to steal the hope from our hearts, we look tenaciously heavenward. Faith and hope anchor our soul, and with a God-strengthened reach, we lay hold of the unseen through faith. Our voices arise through that dark cloud of unknowing as a trumpet sound before the throne of God as we declare our love for Him in the midst of suffering. While yet on the cross, before the vindication of resurrection, we join Jesus and say with a heart of unyielding love, "Into your hand I commit my spirit."

We have one moment on the earth to touch this great place of the Lamb's heart. For all eternity future, we will know Him in His glory, in His beauty. We will drink from the River of Pleasures and know the fullness of joy. Yet the tears will be gone. When the Bridegroom is with us, we will no longer mourn (Matt. 9:15). The times of hope without sight will be memories (Rom. 8:24). The pain of believing without seeing will be over. Faith and hope will stay

> INTIMACY CANNOT REACH ITS FULLNESS WITHOUT SHARED SUFFERING.

behind while the *Love that remains* will escort us into the ages to come (1 Cor. 13:13). The fellowship of suffering remains in the realm of time, yet its fruit will be taken in for all eternity. This fruit will be bright shining jewels adorning our crowns. "...And if children, then heirs— heirs of God and joint heirs of Christ, if indeed we suffer with Him, that we may also be glorified together" (Rom. 8:17).

If we say, "Yes," to this fellowship of suffering, we will one day gaze upon the very real scars upon the Lamb's hands, feet and side with understanding. There will be a memory of intimacy in our gaze and a living understanding in our spirit. Intimacy cannot reach its fullness without shared suffering. Even in the natural, the sweetest love is that which has withstood the winds of adversity together. So, too, with our Beloved Jesus. This dynamic of intimacy originated in His heart. He has given each person many invitations along his or her way to know Him in this chosen communion. He is after the fullness of love. He waits for our voluntary choice to encounter Him in these places. With perfect knowledge and unmatched leadership, He arranges our earthly lives with these doorways strategically positioned along our way. As we learn to recognize that these opportunities are invitations into deeper love, we will seize them with all our hearts. We will cry out with Paul, "…The sufferings of this present time are not worthy to be compared with the glory which shall be revealed in me" (Rom. 8:18).

"I Believe in What is Unseen"

"How easily," my heart says, "I have spent my strength for nothing and in vain." Yet I believe in what is unseen. My pain night and day is that I believe in what is unseen. I believe in a fire that burns within me—transforming me from glory to glory. I believe in strength that is not of this world, welling up and forming within me. I believe in the power of barren prayers and unseen tears. I believe in the Holy Spirit ever abiding within me. All unseen realities.

I wait for You. I am still waiting for You. Oh, how You test my soul with Your tarrying. Yet what choice have I? There is no movement forward without You. So here I wait. How you ruin the lives of Your beloved ones with a love that cannot be argued away and a faith that is an immovable Rock in the journey's way. I do not remain in this place of waiting because my heart is noble, but I wait because my love and my faith have become greater than I and I cannot convince them to depart from me. They are towers that have risen within me and now are indeed the strength of my city. I cannot move them for they are my essence. No longer portions of me but all of me. They are God Himself within me.

All I can do is wait. My soul waits for You. More than the watchmen wait for the morning, I wait for You. My eyes search the horizon for any sign of first light. Surely, You will come. I believe in what is unseen. Surely, You will come to me.

"But as for me, my prayer is to You,
O Lord, in the acceptable time;
O God, in the multitude of Your mercy,
Hear me in the truth of Your salvation.
Deliver me out of the mire, and let me not sink...
Let not the floodwater overflow me,
Nor let the deep swallow me up;
And let not the pit shut its mouth on me.
Hear me, O Lord, for Your lovingkindness is good;
Turn to me according to the multitude of Your tender mercies.
And do not hide Your face from Your servant,
For I am in trouble;
Hear me speedily...
The humble shall see this and be glad;
And you who seek God,
Your hearts shall live.
For the Lord hears the poor,
And does not despise His prisoners"
(Ps. 69: 13-17; 32-33).

CHAPTER 10

PRISONERS OF HOPE

"'...I will set your prisoners free from the waterless pit. Return to the stronghold, you prisoners of hope. Even today I declare that I will restore double to you'" (Zech. 9:11-12).

Seasons of divine silence are the prison sentences that He gives us to pass through while in the boundaries of time. They are noiseless times of stillness that God brings us through not for punishment but for refinement of our faith, hope and love. He imprisons us within "waterless pits." These are the kind of depths that keep the prisoner deep in their yawn yet still with the hope of deliverance. They are too dry to drown us and yet too deep to easily escape. Though God gives them permission to hold us for a time, they are not allowed to kill us, and this hope of deliverance keeps us alive throughout the duration of our sentence. We are alive and well even in the deep of this designated darkness. The Lord's message to us in these times is that He Himself will set us free from the waterless pit in His perfect timing. He calls us a "prisoner of hope" as we wait for Him because our one hope within this cell is anchored in Him: that He would come and show Himself as our Deliverer.

One of the scariest things about these prisons is that only one Person knows where we are. We are tied up and helpless in the deep of a pit, and only one Man knows our exact location. Though we may try a thousand times, we cannot explain its darkness to others. Though we yearn to leave our loneliness, no man is aloud to find us here and deliver us. There are no visiting hours. We're not allowed the comfort of company in these prisons, for they are reserved for God and the soul. Though we try to let others in, most always, our prison walls keep us from the ability to bring them in through words or descriptions. Though we cry out, our voice is quickly swallowed by the silencing shadows. Only one Man knows where we are. One Person has led us here, and He alone can free us once again. He alone knows the pit in which we are held captive, and His voice alone will break open the doorway of freedom. Salvation belongs to the Lord (Ps. 3:8), and He is jealous to be the One who deliverers it to our door.

> *ALL OF HIS WAYS ARE LOVE, AND THEREFORE, WE ARE CONFIDENT THAT HE HAS NOT BROUGHT US HERE FOR PUNISHMENT OR NEGLECT BUT ONLY FOR GREATER LOVE.*

Our comfort in these times rests solely in our knowledge of God's heart. Yes, He is the only One who knows our whereabouts, yet He Himself is also the supreme Deliverer of all time, and surely He will come and deliver His chosen one. He will not leave us here. He will come for us. All of His ways are love, and therefore, we are confident that He has not brought us here for punishment or neglect but only for greater love. When the Lord gives the invitation of suffering and endurance, the end intended by Him is that we would enter into the depths of His compassion and mercy (James 5:10-11).We have asked Him to deepen our love and take us into the fullness of all He would give the human heart, and these prison sentences are part of His answer. They are God's agents to produce the love and agreement that we ourselves have longed for. He will surely deliver us the very moment Love's longsuffering has had its full way within us. The only One who knows our whereabouts will not leave us or forsake us. He will come, just like He promised. He will answer our hope with deliverance.

"Prisoner of Hope"

In this prison, sovereignly sentenced by the Lord, my hope anchors itself in God's deep acquaintance with my way. He Himself has put me here. These walls would have no hold on me except that He has given it to them. If I believe myself to be in prison outside of the will of God, because of my own weakness or sin, it is my end. My hope is crushed, and I am no more. Only in believing that He Himself has ordained this sentence as perfect is my heart sustained. I am God's prisoner. It is His sovereignty that I hope in.

It is through the lens of love that any captivity can be endured. My heart lives today because I believe that His silence is His answer to awaken my heart in greater love. My sustaining hope is that beyond these walls lies the intimacy and union that I have longed for, and my only way through is this dark and silent passage. This prison is indeed my way forward into my inheritance of Love's communion.

Oh, the love-hate relationship I share with these walls. I despise the silent accusation these walls hover over me with, saying, "You will never be free from this place. Silence is your lot in this life. You are not just passing through—these walls are your journey's end." It is enough to drive me mad—the silent accusation of these walls. Perhaps the greatest madness is the life-threatening voice that says, "You're not in prison at all. This freedom is as free as you'll be. This is as good as it gets. You're not a prisoner—you're a free one who just can't taste the freedom." Oh, the madness this lie torments me with.

And yet these walls I love. For they may be devilish, but they are God's devil. In the mysteries of my God's great heart, He has ordained that suffering would often be the escort and pain the companion into the realm of greater love. Along the journey of every believer's way are dark nights and deep, waterless pits. They are cruel and tormenting in nature, yet only through their darkened doors can one enter into the glorious, unutterable intimacy for which we were created. And for this reason, I strangely love these walls.

I love them not in the sense of remaining within them. Oh, I despise the thought. No, everyday I cry out for my release from their captivity. I have every intention of leaving them victoriously behind me and never returning to their darkened womb. Yet at the end of a prisoner's day, after crying out for deliverance all the long hours, I rest in God's usage of these walls. For I know that they have been sovereignly erected around me for the purpose of freedom, not captivity. They boast of being an iron tomb of confinement, yet in truth they are doorways. They think themselves to be the great conquerors over me, and yet His ways are so much higher. He turns a prison wall into the grand gateway of a king. What the enemy means for captivity, God means for freedom.

These prison walls above all believe themselves to be silencers. Lock the prisoner within, and the prisoner's voice is no more. Yet in Your inexpressible wisdom, O God, from the womb of the prison comes the song of deliverance. What the enemy means for silence, You mean for song. "Bring my soul out of prison, that I may praise Your name" (Ps. 142). From the deep and horrible pit comes forth the new song that causes many to fear and put their trust in You (Ps. 40). You bring my soul up from the grave to the end that my glory may sing praise to You and not be silent (Ps. 30). Yes, these prison walls may silence for a night, but a shout of joy comes in the morning, and what my enemy meant for silence, God has ordained for song.

The Hope that Sustains

"...But hope that is seen is not hope; for why does one still hope for what he sees? But if we hope for what we do not see, we eagerly wait for it with perseverance" (Rom. 8:24-25).

We hope in what we cannot see, and our faith is the proof that what is unseen is truly real. The hope within us is Christ in us, our hope of glory (Col. 1:27). It is an ever-abiding reality, anchoring our soul to eternity. As waves tossed to and fro by the sea, we would be if we were not forever fastened to the God unseen. As we find ourselves in the prison sentences of the Lord, this hope has gone ahead of us, entering the Presence behind the veil. There it lives as a true reality, with our very souls attached to it.

Jesus has brought Himself to the low place of earth by setting eternity in the hearts of men, and He has brought weak human beings such as ourselves to the *highest place* by making a way for us to be seated with Him in heavenly places. The One who is our Mediator, who ascended before us, passed through the heavens and took His seat at the right hand of the Father. Fully God. Fully Man. The God-Man. He is the Lamb in the midst of the throne (Rev. 5:6). Who can fathom the possibility that the One who is seated upon the throne is one like us, a MAN? And yet He is also the God of the whole earth. He is the God-Man Jesus Christ. He is the One who is ever interceding for us and bringing us forth in this journey of wholehearted love. After His ascension, when He took His place at the right hand of the Father, He sent forth His Holy Spirit to dwell within us.

HOPE IS THE COMPANION OF OUR HEARTS THAT KEEPS US SUSTAINED IN TIMES OF DARKNESS.

This indwelling One is the Hope that we have as an anchor of our souls (Heb. 6:19). In the deep of the darkest place, we have a living flame of fire within us anchoring us to the fiery Man Himself, and by this we know that He will once again come to us and unite us to Himself. "Now hope does not disappoint, because the love of God has been poured out in our hearts by the Holy Spirit who was given to us" (Rom. 5:5). He is bringing us to Himself that we might be with Him where He is for all eternity (Jn. 17:24). We are joined to Him even in this age where we do not see Him, and He has given us this living hope of His indwelling Spirit as a guarantee (2 Cor. 1:22).

Hope is the companion of our hearts that keeps us sustained in times of darkness. When all around us dims to blackness, and we quiver alone in the pit He has provided, this hope lifts its flaming head. Its eyes see past the realm of circumstance and lift its gaze beyond all temporary walls, to the One who sits upon the throne. There it anchors itself until the day when it is no longer needed, as our eyes finally see the One in whom our soul loves and hope is forever exchanged for sight.

Hope Deferred

"Hope deferred makes the heart sick, but when the desire comes, it is a tree of life" (Prov. 13:12).

Hope, the one that sustains us, is also the one who sickens our hearts when it is deferred. Its continual insistence is known to cause more pain than joy. Yet this is the pain that keeps the soul from the deadened state of unbelief. It is a reasonable sickness for the patient who finds himself in this waiting room of God, the Eternal Surgeon of the soul. He is actually causing health to our beings by giving us the remedy of hope.

Though it weighs heavily upon us, this hope keeps us alive. The "life" it brings to us is very different than what we have ever known. It is the kind of life one feels when to be dead seems more appealing. The one who harbors this hope is the one who has received the invitation to weep each day in the anguish of a believer rather than allow his soul to die in unbelief. This hope is an inward disturbance that refuses us the comfort of giving up. It keeps us alive by the warring of our members and the wrestling with truth that it provokes.

Hope in God, in its deferred state, is as a sickness that gnaws within. But when the longing is answered, and the desire comes, we find in the place of this sickness a healthy tree of life. It is like what Jesus said of Lazarus; this sickness is not unto death, but for the glory of God (Jn. 11:4). This hope that dehabilitates the normalcy of life is not an end in itself. It is a sickness unto something greater —a triumphant tree of life.

"Hope Alive"

Hope. For me it is a painful reality. Perhaps, my dearest friend in this season. For I am indeed a prisoner of hope. Yet hope does not always come dressed in celebration clothes or happy attire. Just when I am about to settle into a dreary, yet comfortable place of unbelief, hope returns to take away every ounce of my fictitious rest, and I am once again caught up in a place of desperately crying out for the promises of God. Without hope, I could abandon every promise forgetfully behind me. But hope anchors me to a realm unseen. Hope continually draws me upward while every accusation pulls me down toward the darkness of this prison. If it were not for a living hope, I could hang pictures on these prison walls and make it my home forever. But hope keeps me ever rattling at the door. Hope keeps me crying out for what my eyes cannot see and my mind can rarely imagine. I hope for my release. I hope that the promises are true. I hope in what lies beyond these walls. I hope in a delivering God that sets the captives free. I hope in a God who created seasons that are ever changing. Will He not also change this season of mine?

In my pain, some might think, I have lost my hope. Really, it is hope that keeps my heart alive. My pain is proof that my heart has not yet died. Within these prison walls, one still cries, one still weeps, one still cries out for release. One is still alive. It is my only option. To live satisfied in this prison would be to live as though dead. To become accustomed to this silence and adapt to these walls would be to live a hopeless life. I am a prisoner of hope. Hope gives me eyes into the outer world...into the world beyond...the unseen realm. Hope keeps me alive.

When hope lives in a lover's heart, even if her lover is taken far from her, with a promise never to return, she is tormented night and day...never able to fully let him go. When hope is alive, pain is present, as well as life. For one cannot go on with life as usual, forgetting the cherished possibility. Hope ruins any such option. Every day she searches the horizon for any sign of her beloved. This hope is life and this hope is pain. Every day she waits for his return...perhaps fainting in heart...still always hoping. Weeping at the close of another day without him. She weeps because in her heart of hearts, hope remains and will not leave her unaccompanied.

I am a prisoner of hope. In this prison, I am kept alive because of a living hope. Everyday I search my horizon for any sign of my Beloved. Yes, there are days when that hope wears bright eyes and a smile; but most days it wears a gnawing ache and many tears. Yet always it keeps my heart alive—ever rattling at the door, ever crying out for deliverance. Hope, my companion. Hope, my friend. Hope...ever keeping my heart alive.

"To everything there is a season,
A time for every purpose under heaven:
A time to be born, and a time to die;
A time to plant, and a time to pluck what is planted;
A time to kill, and a time to heal;
A time to break down, and a time to build up;
A time to weep, and a time to laugh;
A time to mourn, and a time to dance;
A time to cast away stones, and a time to gather stones;
A time to embrace, and a time to refrain from embracing;
A time to gain, and a time to lose;
A time to keep, and a time to throw away;
A time to tear, and a time to sew;
A time to keep silence, and a time to speak;
A time to love, and a time to hate;
A time for war, and a time of peace"
(Eccl. 3:1-8).

CHAPTER 11

SEASONS OF RELEVANCE

One day, we will all stand together on the sea of glass like crystal and, with one voice like the sound of many waters and mighty thunderings, proclaim, "'Let us be glad and rejoice and give Him glory, for the marriage of the Lamb has come, and His wife has made herself ready'" (Rev. 19:7). On that day, we will see many things that are difficult for us to see now—one of which will be the relevance of each individual season that the Lord brought us through, from small to great. We will look with wonder at the times we thought were meaningless and see the grandeur of their significance in the wide scope of God's call upon our lives. We will look with new eyes at the times of suffering and hardship and see their eternal worth, far more than gold. We will gasp to see what He was forming in us even in the dullest of days. Even the times that we thought were utter loss because of our own failure, God will redeem and give beauty for ashes (Is. 61:3).

Our responsibility was simply to say, "Yes," to Him and to agree with the leadership of Jesus over our lives—even when we did not understand His ways. It is the days, the weeks, the months and all of their contents that prepare us for the Lamb of God. These are the tools of God that make us ready. And on that final day, we will see the wonders that the handiwork of God formed in our lives because of our small "yes's" to Him all along the way. He will bring forth a bride made ready.

This is why *each* season is so relevant. Whether the most glorious, the most difficult or the most barren, each has a noble assignment before the throne of God. Not one is extra or merely a pointless period without any value. Each is carefully arranged to bring us into the fullness that God desires for us.

What the Lord asks of us is that we would say, "Yes," and agree with His leadership though we may not have any comprehension of what He is cultivating in these different times. He invites us to come into agreement with Him based upon our knowledge that all of His ways are Love. We know that no matter the season, He is always desiring to reveal His love for us in deeper ways and to bring forth mature love in our own hearts. When we know that Love is always the objective, we can say, "Yes," to whatever the process.

The Seasons of Winter and Spring

In the seasons of the spiritual life, we experience both the winter and the spring. How necessary are each of these extremes. The spring is for *discovering*. The winter is for *remembering*. In the time of spring, God releases the south winds from their holding place, and we run about the hills to find the budding flowers and drink in the fragrance of every finding. We discover new things in His heart, and He unfolds new revelations of His personality to us. We feed on revelation and drink from the wells of impartation. We find out who He is and what He is like, this One we have given ourselves to. We fall in love. Our souls are saturated with abundance and sustained by every good thing from His heart. *In the spring, there is movement.* Frozen waters give way to trickling streams. Solid earth yields to tiny breakthroughs of green life. *What was hidden becomes seen and what was still begins to stir* (Song Sol. 2:11 – 13).

In the winter, we remember. We brood over all the discoveries and all the findings. They become our precious friends for the journey. They are our food and our vision. They become as the picture of the loved one in the prisoner's hand. So gazed upon and cried over that the edges are tattered and the faces smudged. We remember His love (Song Sol. 1:4) and the revelations of Himself that He gave to us in the fruitful times become etched upon our hearts forever. We believe by faith what we cannot now see with our eyes. We recall what we can no longer feel. We ponder

> *IN THE SPRING, THERE IS MOVEMENT. WHAT WAS HIDDEN BECOMES SEEN AND WHAT WAS STILL BEGINS TO STIR*

over the yesterdays and fill our meditation with the goodness He has revealed in times past. In the winter, while the surface sleeps, the budding plants begin to grow deep roots beneath the ground. "I sleep, but my heart is awake…" (Song Sol. 5:2). In the cold winds, we warm our hearts by the living memory of all that we know of our Beloved from seasons past.

In the wintertime, our options are few. We hang on for dear life to what is true. We believe. We believe. We believe. We fix our gaze on what is unseen and trust in the God of the seasons to one day bring the new day. We lean back into the unseen left arm of God (Song Sol. 2:5) and trust in the sovereignty that leads our lives. We hope in the One who constantly causes movement in the Spirit even when there is only stillness in the natural. We remember that our frozenness is never too severe for the sovereign thawing of God. He will come. As surely as He always breaks nature's winter with His warmth, He will come.

When the Lord finally brings us out of the place of winter's cold and into a place of warmth and blessing, we face perhaps a greater test than we knew in our frozenness: the test not of our weakness but of our strength. When weakness and pain are ever raging, so too is the constant reach of our soul towards God, our Deliverer. We don't have to tell ourselves to cry out to God, for the cry is already rising before we wake in the morning and the last one to grow quiet at the end of the day. Yet when the grippings of our utter inability are loosened and the darkness of the night is dispersed, a whole new swirl of the enemies-of-life lift their heads. No longer kept in the safety of our prison walls, we are once again exposed to all the options that a free man knows. With the poverty that we knew in our

IN THE WINTER TIME, OUR OPTIONS ARE FEW. WE HANG ON FOR DEAR LIFE TO WHAT IS TRUE...WE FIX OUR GAZE ON THE UNSEEN...

prison sentence only a memory, we now face the great test of *freedom* and *prosperity*.

David well expressed the tension of these transitions:

> I will extol You, O Lord, for You have lifted me up, and have not let my foes rejoice over me. O Lord my God, I cried out to You, and You healed me. O Lord, You brought my soul up from the grave; You have kept me alive, that I should not go down to the pit. Sing praise to the Lord, you saints of His, and give thanks at the remembrance of His holy name. For His anger [chastisement] is but for a moment, His favor is for life; weeping may endure for a night, but joy comes in the morning. *Now in my prosperity I said, "I shall never be moved." Lord, by Your favor You have made my mountain stand strong* (Ps. 30:1-7, emphasis added).

His cry arose to the Lord when the chastisement of God was upon him. The Lord answered him and delivered him from trouble. Now in prosperity, he proclaims that he will not be moved. Now when life flows once again, he says, "I will be held steadfast even in the test of abundance."

> THESE "SOUTH WINDS" OF PROSPERITY ARE JUST AS CRUCIAL TO US AS THE "NORTH WINDS" OF SEVERITY.

These "south winds" of prosperity are just as crucial to us as the "north winds" of severity. If such a relevance is true of our prison sentences, than that same relevance applies to our days of freedom and abundance. The times that we drink of the sweetness of the Lord and taste of His goodness are just as necessary to the soul's maturity as the seasons of bitter testing. The cold winds strip us and the warm winds clothe and restore us. In both times we drink deeply of all that God gives us. In times of weakness, it is the memory of God's enabling strength that sustains our hearts. In times of strength, it is the remembrance of our utter weakness that protects us. While in prison, we cry out to God, "Deliver me, for You alone are my strength!" While in freedom, we exclaim, "Protect me, for when I do not feel my utter weakness, I am prone to forget my constant need of You!"

When the Lord brings us from winter to spring, He feeds our souls with feasts of abundance. Just as we were kept alive by every drop of life He offered us in the time of trouble, we are now restored and renewed by the fountain of rushing water He offers us in the time of fruitfulness. Now we store up for future droughts. For surely the winds will change once again. We will move from knowing prosperity to once more encountering poverty. Thus, nothing can be wasted. In times of famine, we will be sustained by what the Lord stored up within us during the times of plenty.

The deception contained in these more comfortable seasons is just that: *the comfort*. We sink into the easy chair of relief and come under the falsity that we deserve a "break" now that our prison sentence is over. Yet our Beloved God does not shepherd our time on the earth in this way. Every day holds importance and its own account of relevance. There are not "days off" in the Spirit, only different forms of receiving the life He gives. In the bitter testing seasons, we cling to Him as we would cling to the only place of safety in a storm. Now in the warm, sweet seasons, we receive His life and love in the quiet of "peace time" and the romance of renewal.

Just as the winter freeze holds an invitation to trust and believe in the unseen, so too these spring rains hold within them a doorway of invitation. They invite us to not forget the etchings of identity that God drove deep within us in the wintertime and to remember that He alone is our Reward. Our enemy in these times of freedom is our many options. When the south winds are present and all is well, we must guard very carefully against the appeal to comfort our souls with things other than God Himself. A prisoner has but one Person to talk to: God. He has but one thing to do with his time: pray. Yet once free, all the voices rush in and all the opportunities, good and bad, seek to lay hold of his time and energy. Good is always the enemy of the best, and the man now has a far greater chance of losing his heart by secondary pleasures than when he spent his day in a sovereign prison where God was His only comfort and pleasure possible.

When my natural strength is taken from me by the Divine hand of God, I have zero options but to lean only and entirely upon *His* strength. But when it is restored to me, even for the purposes of His will, the test before me is to remember how truly weak I am without His enabling. Though now this weakness is so deeply hidden beneath the surface, I must not imagine that I do not just as severely need the strength of God in all that I do. When my inability is not here to give constant reminder of my neediness for God, I am prone to lean on my own understanding. The key in both winter and spring is to know that in each extreme, He alone is my source of strength. In my prosperity I recognize that I can do nothing apart from Him (Jn. 15:5), and in my poverty I remember that I can do all things through Christ who strengthens me (Phil. 4:13).

Seasons In Between

But what of the seasons that are not necessarily winter, they are neither spring nor summer nor fall? What of those times that are not cold or still enough to be winter nor sweet and animated enough to be spring? They are neither sufficiently hot and bold enough to be summer nor colorful and friendly enough to be fall. Their definitions are blurred, and they lie somewhere in between the periods that we can box in with understanding. Because of their unwillingness to be categorized, we tend to want to push through them and be rid of them quickly for fear that they were never intended to show up and that they are but a meaningless detour on our way. Yet this is not the case. They are neither meaningless nor a diversion from our way but deeply essential.

> IN MY PROSPERITY I RECOGNIZE THAT I CAN DO NOTHING APART FROM HIM (JN. 15:5), AND IN MY POVERTY I REMEMBER THAT I CAN DO ALL THINGS THROUGH CHRIST WHO STRENGTHENS ME (PHIL. 4:13).

Tucked right in between our most extreme and intense seasons, whether the darkened night times or the high mountain seasons of Love's exhilaration, these in-between-seasons offer their contribution to our continual movement forward in Love. These are the seasons that fill the pages between the climax points of our personal volumes of life. They are the climb before the mountain top and the descent before the valley floor. They are indeed the journey. So often in our life of prayer, we can perceive relevance in the times of difficulty, and we easily understand the significance of the seasons of victory. Yet in the months and years that lie in between, our hearts are prone to the most discouragement. It is the "in between" periods that leave us most disillusioned.

Their relevance is not guaranteed to reveal itself in this life. We may never understand the gold of these days until the age to come when the Lord pulls back the veil and unlocks their divine job descriptions and purpose. Yet we can rest in their importance simply by the truth that He placed them unavoidably in our path and, therefore, has hidden worth within their chambers. They are menial and mundane to our understandings, and we only wish that we could be rid of them and get onto the real dramas of knowing and loving Him. Yet something about our God loves these blah passages and finds great purpose in their contribution.

In these times, the best way to position the heart is in rest. We rest in the understanding that all His ways are love and even these pathways are part of the package. Our tendency is to waste many a day running about the small cell of these enclosed seasons, rearing our heads into their boundary lines and continually attempting to outrun them. Either we have the response just described, or we sit down in disillusionment and allow doubt to eat away at our belief in God's banner of love over our lives. Either way, we do not believe in their sovereign purpose. We do not recognize the hand of the Lord behind their monotonous walls and, thus, become greatly discouraged within their custody.

The most important thing for us to know and believe is that the Holy Spirit is continually and constantly leading us carefully and strategically forward in our love and our knowledge of God. There is a portion for each season and an invitation within each day. Oh, that we would align our hearts to agree with the preparations He has counted most valuable for us each day and receive whatever it is that He desires to implant in our hearts. Oh, that we would extend the arms of our hearts and cry, "Have Your way O God! Have Your way in me. Whatever You desire to give me in this time, have Your way! I trust You with the seasons. My times are in Your hands!"

> *WE DO NOT RECOGNIZE THE HAND OF THE LORD BEHIND THEIR MONOTONOUS WALLS AND, THUS, BECOME GREATLY DISCOURAGED WITHIN THEIR CUSTODY.*

All the seasons are indeed bringing us into greater love. All the passages and parts of the journey are unto the fullness of knowing the height and width and depth and length of God's knowledge-surpassing love. Love does not have an end. It is endless for it is contained within the infinite and everlasting God. Yet He is leading each lover of Himself into the utter consumption of Divine Love. We cannot know Love's end, but we *can* find our *own* end in its all-consuming embrace.

A Prayer to Respond Rightly

I must pay attention in this time. O Lord, help me pay attention. I want to give myself to these winds as a student of Your ways with me. Help me to discern Your ways with me. Help me to give the corresponding response to the intensity of this season. For surely it will come and go. When that transition takes place, I want to have moved with the winds in fullness and to have drunk deeply of the cup of this season. I must pay attention. Help me God to pay attention.

For some time I have looked for this season. I have searched the horizon for the sign of first light. I have sat alone in silence awaiting the faintest sound of the coming rain. And here I am. The winds have changed. The new day has begun to show its face. The silence has drifted away to its holding place for later seasons. And I am here being swept gracefully to and fro in this gentle whirlwind. I am in movement. Oh, help me to respond rightly in this time.

You have tested my soul. You tested me with Your absence. You tested me with Your silence. You tested me with the merciless ache of utter stillness. You made me a student of the night season, a watchman waiting for the morning. You made me sensitive to every whisper of the waking dawn. Oh, let me not forget one shade of what the shadows taught me. Let me not rush about in movement now that You have restored my ability to move. I want to move with You. When You are still, I am still. When You dance, I dance. When You rush, I rush. But let me never move for the sake of movement.

I am Your garden, reserved for Your pleasure. I am no longer mine, gladly. I am Yours. I desire that You would blow upon my garden that its spices might flow out. I am reserved for Your pleasure. In the silent seasons of the north winds and the movement seasons of the south. I am Yours. If south winds now rest upon my soul, then enjoy me now as You enjoyed me in the cold bitter winds of testing. I cling to You. I know what it is to sink into the winter's frost. I cannot afford to not drink every drop of this season to the fullness of its wealth. Help me God for You know my weakness. Let me pay attention in this time. Let me not slumber in the refreshment of this season. Let me respond rightly. Help me to respond rightly. Oh, give me the grace to respond rightly.

"Consumed"

Human heart, small and weak, open me, Lord,
So tenderly
Eyes uplifted to eternity, unveil them, Lord,
That I might see
Let Your truth open up Love's door
And where my heart is too small, wound me more
Do not stop where my love runs dry
But increase the river that I might fly
Limit not my heart to what it can hold
But enlarge my soul to love You more
What will You give to the human heart
If You would give all You desire and no less?
This I plead for my own heart
Give all You desire me to possess
Do not end with a flickering fire—
Let flames consume my all
Take me further than Love's edge—
Immerse body mind and soul
All that is in Your heart to give, This I ask of You
As much as the human heart can receive,
Envelop, Immerse and Consume

CHAPTER 12

CONSUMED IN LOVE'S FIRE

"Set me as a seal upon your heart, as a seal upon your arm; for love is as strong as death, jealousy as cruel as the grave; its flames are flames of fire, a most vehement flame. Many waters cannot quench love, nor can floods drown it. If a man would give for love all the wealth of his house, it would be utterly despised" (Song Sol. 8:6-7).

The journey of the heart does not ever reach an ending point. For all of eternity it continues as Love increases and unfolds. We move through the phases and seasons of God's embrace, the dance of intimacy, until we finally see His face. And then for all the ages to come, Love will unfold and unfold in the abundance of its full extent. Our lives on the earth are but the womb of the life to come, and only *then* is our real destiny realized in its glory. Yet even in this life, there is a certain *fullness* offered to the human heart by God, and it is that wealth in its entirety that we are after. My question to the Lord has been about what it looks like when a heart comes to the place of total possession by God in this womb of the present age. What does it look like when a soul is utterly *owned* by God? When God created the earth and set man upon it, knowing that he would live a life of 70 to 80 years at most and then forever in eternity with Him, what was the highest desire found in the heart of God for the soul of that man? What does a heart on the earth aflame with the love of God look like in full blaze? When God awakens desire in our hearts and then takes us on a journey of holy desire for all of our days, what is the portrait of our final breaths? We know that for every heart this picture varies. The beautiful artwork of God is manifested in so many diverse displays and seen differently in every individual union between God and each heart. And though every representation will have its own tone and quality, I believe there are some general considerations to be known and comprehended about what this place of Love's maturity in this life looks like.

I believe that the all-embracing portrait of the one given fully to God is recognized by the complete burning up of that person with Love's ardent flame. It is the sealing of God's fiery love upon his heart (Song Sol. 8:6). This is where He is bringing each one—into the full consumption of His burning affection. We are seared by that which remains for all eternity. We are caught up, taken captive and gloriously swept into this eternal fire of divine devotion. No longer our own, we belong to Another. We are hidden with Christ only to be revealed when He is revealed. The fire of Love has taken us willingly and eagerly captive, and we have made our home in its eternal burnings. No longer is any sacrifice too great or any reward held in higher importance than the reward of the love of Christ. Without a thought, we would give for Love all the wealth of our house and all our possessions, utterly despising any recognition of our sacrifice (Song Sol. 8:7). As Paul declared, "Yet indeed I count all things loss for the excellence of the knowledge of Christ Jesus my Lord, for whom I have suffered the loss of all things, and count them as rubbish, that I may gain Christ." (Phil. 3:8). This is where the Lord is taking each heart who has offered his life to this holy pursuit. And oh, that God would give us the immeasurable grace to live long in this place before we see Him face to face! Oh, that we would live as men and women of whom the world was not worthy because of the utter devotion that defines our lives!

This place of mature Love is also the point of no return. When we are so gripped and possessed by Love's passion, we have crossed over into the place where we could never again return to what previously gave us pleasure outside of Him. Peter had arrived at this place when Jesus asked him if he wished to leave Him due to His heavy teaching. He said to Jesus, "'Lord, to whom shall we go? You have the words of eternal life'" (Jn. 6:68). The truth is that we have left behind our former ways. We have come to the place where we have nothing to return to, for we have long ago made Jesus the one Reward of our hearts and lives. We cry out with the psalmist, "Whom have I in heaven but You? And there is none on the earth that I desire besides You. My flesh and my heart fail; but God is the strength of my heart and my portion forever" (Ps. 73:25-26).

He is bringing us into this wholeheartedness and nothing less. To be consumed by His love is to be unified in heart, mind, soul and strength. Within this flaming chamber, our lives are utterly consumed by the one thing we have desired. We are not divided from Him in this place. To find a heart so captured is to also find the Lord Jesus for nothing separates us from His love. We are bound by Love, and it holds so fierce a grip on us that even death and the grave and all the many waters will not break loose the grasp (Song Sol. 8:6-7). Oh, how we need this fire of God to possess our souls! Jesus said, "'I came to send fire on the earth, and how I wish it were already kindled!'" (Lk. 12:49). The God-Man with fire in His eyes gazes upon each of our hearts with desire to bring us into this baptism of fire (Lk. 3:16). He wills to consume each voluntary heart with His ardent affection and to bring forth from humanity living flames of love.

The Sting of the Fire

We are afraid to be wholehearted and for obvious reasons. The fear of the fire is due to the truth that God is nothing short of all consuming. He is not a God of fractions. There is no middle ground within the fullness of Love. There is no grey area to linger in within wholeheartedness. We fear total abandonment because we fear Him. And it is right that we should fear Him, for the fear of the Lord *is* the beginning of wisdom (Prov. 1:7). Yet let us not allow this fear of the Lord to drive us from Him but to compel us to Him. Would I not rather dwell in the center of the Almighty Whirlwind than peer from outer limits at its unlimited power? And would it not be better to dwell with Everlasting Burnings (Is. 33:14) than to stand far from Him and resist His consuming nature? Is it not preferable to voluntarily plunge myself into the depths of Love's Ocean than to stand on the shore as if I had the ability to avoid its imminent engulfing? I would rather live within this Ocean of incomprehensible affection and dwell with Everlasting Burnings than live at a distance and take the risk of my distance giving way to offense toward Him. Surely, this weighty choice is my security. For though I cannot know all that I say, "Yes," to, I know I say, "Yes," to Love. And I know that wherever He may lead me, I am forever kept in Love's embrace. I know that intimacy is my protection and the seal upon my heart (Song Sol. 8:6).

The sting of the fire is also found in our unlikeness to Him. "Who among us shall dwell with the devouring fire? Who among us shall dwell with everlasting burnings?" (Is. 33:14). It is the one who walks righteously. The pure in heart shall see Him. And it is when we remain within the Refiner's Fire that we are cured of our ailments and even brought into the place of utter health of soul. In order to know and dwell with this Devouring Fire, we must willingly surrender all false understandings of Him. We come as blank pages for Him to write upon. With sincere hearts we cry out, "Write Your name upon my forehead! (Rev. 7:3). Set Your seal upon my heart!" (Song Sol. 8:6). We are driven by the very real

> *THE STING OF THE FIRE IS ALSO FOUND IN OUR UNLIKENESS TO HIM. WHO AMONG US SHALL DWELL WITH THE DEVOURING FIRE?*

ardor of His love, and this love has led us to the place that we could have never reached in our own strength and strivings. Enjoyment has equipped us for this resolute abandonment. We have become lovesick bond-servants. Slaves of holy desire. We have surrendered to the living Flame of Love. And surely our eyes shall see the King in His beauty within the glowing brightness of this blaze (Is. 33:15).

Yet another reason for our fear of the fire of the Lord is because this God of ours is so seemingly unsafe. He is dangerous and unpredictable. He plays by no human rules, only His own. Total abandonment to Him is a reckless expedition with an uncertain destination. We have no idea what He will do with us if we surrender all to Him. These are understandable responses but false nonetheless. We are fools to think ourselves safe outside of this flame. Though He is all consuming and though our unlikeness to Him makes us not understand His ways, He is our one and only hiding place. Though He is dangerous in the sense that we do not know where He will lead us, truly the greater danger is to not be lead utterly and entirely by Him. We will not find a "no man's land" in this journey. We either fling ourselves into this highest Flame or lose our very souls to all lesser flames. To be consumed by the Love of God is really our only choice of wisdom.

WE EITHER FLING OURSELVES INTO THIS HIGHEST FLAME OR LOSE OUR VERY SOULS TO ALL LESSER FLAMES.

The Heights and Depths of Love's Consumption

"…That you, being rooted and grounded in love, may be able to comprehend with all the saints what is the width and length and depth and height – to know the love of Christ which passes knowledge; that you may be filled with the fullness of God" (Eph. 3:17-19).

We were made for the fullness of God, the fullness of Love—a never-ending pursuit. Within this fullness is the incomprehensible heights, depths, the lengths and the widths of love. We have looked thus far at the communion with the Lord in the heights of sweet intimacy. As He seizes our hearts with His magnificent closeness, He takes us to the heights of enjoyment and satisfaction in His word. He brings us to the mountain-tops and wins our hearts forever by the divine pleasure. He takes us up into the joy of experiencing Him in communion and romances us by revealing His delight in us. We are brought into the glorious river of His affections in prayer. Oh, the wonderful heights of God's love! The fellowship! The satisfaction! Yet this is only part of Love's communion. Along with the heights come also the depths…

When we began on this journey, we had so many glorious aspirations and imagined that our way forward would be a continual ascension—a never-ending climb to higher heights of divine pleasure. We had envisioned an ever-increasing rise from glory to glory. And it is, in once sense. It is only that we do not have an understanding of the heart of Jesus and what He has defined as glorious. In our sincere but still immature understandings, we assumed that our journey would simply continue in this ascent into greater and greater enjoy-ment. Isn't that what only makes sense—that pleasure would only rise into higher and higher exhilaration until the day we finally see His face? Once again, this is true, in a sense, but not as we imagined. We are in for a surprise, a very perplexing surprise.

We soon begin to discover the vast difference between what we had envisioned our voyage into greater Love to look like from how He has actually planned it. As we move from the introductions of intimacy to the place of maturity, we find that He is truly moving us to complete abandonment and, surpris-ingly, that is far more painful than we had imagined. We are surprised to find that with the heights of Love come the *depths* of Love. With the south winds come the *north* winds and with the mountain tops come the *valleys*. With the power of the resurrection comes the fellowship of suffering.

WITH EVERY STEP NEARER TO HIM, OUR ROMANTIC PRESUMPTIONS GIVE WAY TO REVEAL THE TRUE JOURNEY INTO KNOWING THE HEART OF THE LAMB OF GOD.

With every step nearer to Him, our romantic presumptions give way to reveal the true journey into knowing the heart of the Lamb of God. Is He not still the Lamb who stands as though slain in the midst of the throne (Rev. 5:6)? Is He not still the One who has borne our griefs and carried our sorrows (Is. 53:4)? And is there not even now a fellowship to be known in His sufferings (Phil. 3:10) and a deeper consolation to be found in that place? Though in the beginning, we were wooed, wowed and stunned by the ascensions of Love's measure, the deeper we go in intimacy with the Lamb of God, it is the declensions of Love that soon direct our journey.

It is once again intimacy that He is after in this invitation. He is not asking us to go somewhere that He has not Himself already gone. He is not giving a cross that is not itself encompassed in the greater Cross. He invites us to the fellowship of suffering that we might know the full measure of intimacy's embrace. That full measure cannot be known in the heights alone. It is the depths that complete the fullness. He is jealous that we would know Him in this place. As we partake of the suffering, we begin to partake of the consolations there found (2 Cor. 1:7).

We have said, "Yes," to Him and to His fullness, no matter what the cost. Now, He takes us into places we did not know were part of Love, and when we think we must finally be nearing the ocean floor, He takes us deeper still. Our hearts cry, "How deep will this river take me? How far are we declining Jesus?" We are bewildered to find that as the miles of deep and dangerous Ocean continue, and the fellowship of His suffering increases, there is no apology from the Lord. What we consider to be "too much" and "too difficult" He does not make amends for. He is neither surprised nor troubled by their extremity and intensity. This is where Love goes. From the heights of Love's exhilaration to the depths of Love's suffering—that I may know Him in the power of His resurrection and the fellowship of suffering (Phil 2:10).

The one who has asked such a dangerous prayer as "fill me with fullness of God," soon discovers the weight of such request. For the Man with gladness above all His companions is also the Man of suffering. And the depths of Love do not contradict the heights of Love. The Lion is also the Lamb. The King of all became the Servant of all. Oh, the seeming paradoxes in His personality! Oh, the spectrum of His affection! For He not only ascends to a realm unimaginable; He *descends* to a realm unthinkable in His vast love for us. "He who descended is also the One who ascended far above all the heavens, that He might fill all things (Eph. 4:10). In our cry to enter His fullness, we were not disappointed when the Lord brought us up to the heights of exhilaration. When the heights kept rising to greater crescendos, we did not complain. Should we now turn Him away when He continues to answer our cry for fullness by inviting us to the depths of His love? Should we now be offended when the deep of Love keeps giving way to greater depth? The two extremes do not belong in separation. For both height and depth dwell within the heart of the Lamb. They are the two-edged sword that has so' wounded our lovesick hearts. They are inseparable places that do not exist without each other. Without depth, what is height? Without height, who can define the deep? One gives definition and context to the other. When I dance upon the high and

BOTH HEIGHT AND DEPTH DWELL WITHIN THE HEART OF THE LAMB. THEY ARE THE TWO-EDGED SWORD THAT HAS SO WOUNDED OUR LOVESICK HEARTS.

exhilarating mountaintops, I am anchored by the memory of the deep. When I find myself nearly drowning in the suffering Ocean of Love's deep, my soul is upheld by the heights I have known in God.

Oh, the heart of the Lamb of God! The One who is fully God and fully Man holds the fullness of Love within His heart—and that fullness encompasses the tiptop of its height and the rock bottom of its depth. "For you know the grace of our Lord Jesus Christ, that though He was rich, yet for your sakes He became poor, that you through His poverty might become rich" (2 Cor. 8:9). This is the Lamb of God. This is the Bridegroom of all the ages.

The heights of His person we receive readily. He is the King of kings and the Chief among ten thousand. He rules the vast empires of heaven and earth, high and exalted in His glory. His divinity we love, for He vindicates us with His deliverance and crushes our enemies with His power. Yet just as equal to His might is His meekness. Without contradiction in His personality, His greatness and His gentleness abide. The One who ascended to the highest place and was given a name above every name in Heaven and earth is also the One who descended to the lowest place. He became the Servant of all, taking on the sin of the world and bearing the weight of God's wrath. This God-Man encompasses the heights and the depths of Love's extent within His very person. The entire scope of Love is held within the heart of this King. He is just as acquainted with suffering as He is with conquering.

The question to ask is, am I offended by Your meekness? Do I embrace Your prominence and shun

Your lowliness? Have I received Your kingliness and rejected Your servanthood? Have I known Your holiness and not your humiliation? For surely within the vastness of His personality, it is His meekness that we most stumble over. And it is this part of His heart that invites us to His fellowship of suffering. It is the meek Lamb of God who was slain. It is the Man of sorrows that wept alone at Gethsemane.

> *SURELY WITHIN THE VASTNESS OF HIS PERSONALITY, IT IS HIS MEEKNESS THAT WE MOST STUMBLE OVER.*

To know the fullness of this Bridegroom's heart, we must understand the relentless deep that Love took Him to. In this great Ocean we have joined ourselves to, let us not receive the tidal waves and refuse the deep unto deep.

Jesus comes to the maiden in the Song of Solomon and knocks upon her door (Song Sol. 5:2). His head is covered with the dew of the night. He is coming from the Garden of Gethsemane with the same request that He gave to His disciples. He invites her to open for Him and invite Him in. He is inviting her to the fellowship of suffering. I imagine this scene very vividly. He comes not as a warrior and not as a King. He is not the conquering stag upon the mountains (Song Sol. 2:8). His heart is weighty, and His eyes red with weeping in unutterable sorrow. She could have said to Him, "Jesus, You look so different now. I have never seen You look this way. Instead of the conquering King You come to me as the suffering Lamb. Jesus, why are You trembling? What has happened within Your heart to cause such suffering? Where has Love taken You, O God? For surely You have been to a deep I do not know of. Love has cast You to the bottom of the ocean floor, and You have gladly come under its force. O Jesus, Man of sorrows, I have never seen You look this way before."

This is the meek-hearted Lamb. The Man that walked the earth two thousand years ago has not changed. The desire that arose from His heart then, still lives and breathes each day. "'Father, I desire that they...may be with Me where I am...'" (Jn. 17:24). It is this desire that takes Him to depths we have not fathomed. Did He not descend to the depths of hell to overcome all enemies of Love? Yes, we have not yet even touched the understanding of how far and how long and how deep and how wide is the love of Christ. Yet He gives us invitation to know all of these measures. "For to you it has been granted on behalf of Christ, not only to believe in Him, but also to suffer for His sake" (Phil. 1:29). Let us not stop at Love's heights, moving in the power of the resurrection and experiencing the exhilaration of the glories. Let us also respond to His invitation to know the fellowship of the deep places, though they descend so far past where we had imagined they would. For truly we desire to know this Man Christ Jesus in fullness. We want to be friends of the Bridegroom. We desire to stand within His counsel and know His heart. We cannot embrace only a measure of this flaming divine heart. We must say to this great Ocean,

> *LET US NOT STOP AT LOVE'S HEIGHTS...LET US ALSO RESPOND TO HIS INVITATION TO KNOW THE FELLOWSHIP OF THE DEEP PLACES...*

"I have joined myself to You. All that You are I receive."

Divine Possession

"...You were marked in him with a seal, the promised Holy Spirit, who is a deposit guaranteeing our inheritance until the redemption of THOSE WHO ARE GOD'S POSSESSION—to the praise of his glory" (Eph. 1:13, NIV, emphasis added).

The Lord is after the entirety of our heart, soul, mind and strength. He is bringing us to a certain and definite transition in our walk. He is moving us from the place of seeking our own inheritance in Jesus to the place of living as those who are indeed *His* inheritance. He desires that we would begin to know more and more the riches of the glory of His inheritance in us, His saints (Eph. 1:18). We transition from having our main preoccupation being the furtherance of our own pleasure in Him, and we give ourselves to the position of being the pleasured of God—the enjoyment of His own heart. We are His possession (Deut. 32:9, Eph. 1:14), His reward. He brings us to the place where more than anything we desire our Beloved to come to His garden and drink deeply of what He Himself has poured into us, to partake of what He has planted within us. We cry, "Let my Beloved come to His garden and eat its pleasant fruits" (Song Sol. 4:16). We cry out

WE CRY OUT FOR THE FULLNESS OF GOD'S ENJOYMENT OF WHAT HE HAS PLANTED AND TENDED WITHIN US.

for the fullness of God's enjoyment of what He has planted and tended within us.

We make this transition voluntarily. Given our absolute freedom, Love compels us to choose Him and cling to Him as closely as though we were bound to Him. Our wholehearted allegiance belongs to Him, and we know that we are His belonging and His inheritance. We offer ourselves as living sacrifices, holy and acceptable to God (Rom. 12:1). And we wait for the One who answers by fire to come and consume longing sacrifice on the altar we have so lovingly tied ourselves to. Our final ambition is no longer our own satisfaction but *His* satisfaction. We desire that He would find the labor of His soul in us and be satisfied (Is. 53:11). He has desired more than a bride who is exhilarated by Him. His jealousy has claimed within us an eternal spouse that has moved past the place of only receiving His love and into the realm higher, the place where Love so constrains us that we become living sacrifices unto God, laying down our lives for Him. We are servants and prisoners to Love's flame.

We see lives of such shining brilliance all through history and even in our day—lives of whom the world was not worthy...so consumed, so conquered in love for this Man Jesus that they were as people of another world...loving not their lives even unto death, for holy affection so compelled them. Many lives of the Jesus-adoring martyrs throughout history so diffused the fragrant Love of God that those persecuting them repented and surrendered their hearts to Christ by the mere witness of the bondservants' devotion unto

Christ. This is the power of one owned by the Love of God. They are those of another world.

Again, we see this kind of powerful possession when Jesus comes as the suffering Servant to the bride in the Song of Solomon (5:2). Jesus knocks on the door of His bride's heart, inviting her to the fellowship of suffering. She arises to open for Him only to find Him absent. With desperation and a yearning heart, she goes into the night in search for Him. She calls His name, and He does not answer; she searches for Him but she does not find Him. In the midst of her painful search, the watchmen of the city find her and strike her, wounding her deeply. In all her journey prior, she has not yet experienced such a brutal suffering. Her affliction is the combination of her Beloved leaving without warning and the watchmen whom she trusted beating her without just cause.

Oh, the darkness of this night. Here the heart is tested. It is within the deep of this greatest affliction that we hear the sweetest song of the bride's love-conquered heart. We witness the response of one who belongs, body, mind and soul, to the Custodian of Love. She is not her own; she is His. And no wind of adversity could pry her out of Love's grasp. With unmatched devotion, she cries, "If you find my Beloved, tell Him I am lovesick" (Song Sol. 5:8).

In the heat of her adversity, she has but one response. She responds in love. She says to the daughters, in essence, "Give a message to my Beloved if you find Him before I do. Tell Him that my heart is not offended at Him right now. Tell Him that even now in this utter darkness and confusion, holy passion is flowing as a river in my heart. Tell Him that I trust Him right now. Above all else, let Him know that I am lovesick for Him; I am faint with love for Him even now."

Oh, the Love of God that He fills us with! It is as strong as death. Its claims upon the voluntary heart are as severe as the claims that death makes upon the captive body. Its jealousy is as intense as the grave, swallowing up its hostage without the slightest reservation. It creates in a willing heart a masterpiece of fearless abandonment. The severity of physical suffering and even death are reduced to nothing when compared to the severity of the burning passion for God. Jesus' love for us broke through the barrier of death, and this is the very Love that burns within our hearts for Him!! Its flames are flames of fire with flashes of desire

WHEN WE HAVE SURRENDERED TO THE HIGHEST FLAME, OUR HEARTS ARE PROTECTED FROM ALL LESSER FLAMES.

and great vehemence. Oh, the jealous fire of God's Love! It is the fire that we so need to consume our hearts and mark us as His forever. "For I am convinced that neither death nor life, nor angels nor principalities nor powers, nor things present nor things to come, nor height nor depth nor any other created thing, shall be able to separate you from the love of God, which is in Christ Jesus our Lord" (Rom. 8:38-39).

It is in the safety of the "Everlasting Burnings" that our hearts are kept from offense even in the hour of great testing. When we have surrendered to the highest Flame, our hearts are protected from all lesser flames. When we voluntarily give ourselves to be bondservants of love, we are slaves to no one else. We are in truth finally free. When we have submitted to the wound of the Love of God, all lesser wounds have no power over us. When in the perplexities and pains of our afflictions, we will reenact this scene found in the Song of Solomon, having but one response, the response of a lovesick heart!!

In our day, the Lord is giving this invitation. The severities of the times require nothing less than whole-hearted responses. As we near the return of our Beloved Jesus and the end of natural history draws to a close, it is hearts aflame with the love of God that God is bringing forth. He is calling all who will hear to the journey of the burning heart. His invitation is all about Love, and He is the jealous fire of its vehement flames. He desires all of our hearts and not only part. He entreats us to fling ourselves unsparingly into the Ocean of His affections until we are utterly consumed and unrelentingly bound to Him.

The severity of the testing that we as lovers of Jesus will face at the end of the age will be the literal fulfillment of what is illustrated by the Shulamite (Song Sol. 5). In the darkness of the night, the One whom we love will give us invitation to arise and come out to meet Him (Matt. 25:1). With yearning hearts that long for Him, we will arise and follow Jesus into the night. Yet in that hour, our hearts will be refined by testing as we face the delay of the Lord's manifest presence and the harshness of great persecution.

> HE ENTREATS US TO FLING OURSELVES UNSPARINGLY INTO THE OCEAN OF HIS AFFECTIONS...

What will our response be when we find Him gone? And what about when He *allows* us to be persecuted for His sake (Matt. 5:12)? What will arise from our hearts? Will we know His heart? Will our history of intimacy protect us from doubting Him in that hour? Will we have known Him so richly in times past and all the seasons prior that our hearts are preserved from offense? "Blessed is he who is not offended because of Me'" (Matt. 11:6). Will we have so received His love into the chambers of our hearts that its flames consume all lesser flames? Or will our hearts be crushed under the weight of such difficulty and crises? Will His invitation become too radical for us in the midst of the pressures?

Oh, that we would have the ready response of the bride of Christ in that hour…so that as our accusers sneer, "What is your Beloved more than another? Has He not left you? Why does He allow this to happen to you if He loves you as you say He does?"…that we would answer not with simply correct theology, but with a living river of confident affection flowing in our inner man. "Let me tell you about my Beloved. He is beautiful. He is radiant. He is Chief among ten thousand, and His leadership over my life is perfect. Oh, He is dazzling! He is excellent! And all of His ways are just and true! This is my Beloved; this is my Friend."

In the hour that God arises to shake all that can be shaken, He will have many burning ones on the earth with immovable hearts. They are those who have plunged into this Ocean of God's love with violent pursuit. Within us is the everlasting fire of love-that-remains when all else fades. Out of the womb of time will arise our hearts ignited with the passion that maintains its burning flames for eternity. Prisoners of holy devotion, we, as slaves of Love will arise as burning and shining lamps, shamelessly consumed by the Lover of our souls.

ORDER ONLINE

Order online at: www.afterhisheart.com.

For volume discounts, visit the web site.

For orders outside US visit: www.fotb.com/shop/

ORDER BY MAIL

Books	Qty	Price	Total
Deep unto Deep	_____	$12.99	_____
		Subtotal:	_____
	Shipping. Add 10% to subtotal:		
		(Minimum $2.00):	_____
	Tax. (Missouri residents add 7.525%):		_____
	Total Enclosed (US Funds Only):		_____

Your Name: _____

Address: _____

City, State, Zip: _____

Phone Number: _____

E-Mail Address: _____

Make Checks & Money Orders payable to "After His Heart." Send payment with order form to:

> After His Heart
> 4513 E. 112th St.
> Kansas City, MO., 64137

ABOUT THE AUTHOR

Dana Candler is an author, speaker, and instructor at the Forerunner School of Ministry, a full time Bible school affiliated with the International House of Prayer of Kansas City. She and her husband Matt serve full-time as intercessory missionaries at the International House of Prayer, where they have been a part of the leadership team since its beginning in 1999.

The passion of Dana's heart is the subject of *deep intimacy with God* and the *unending quest for the fullness of His love* that we were each created for. Intensifying this passion is her burden regarding the urgency of this present hour of history and the desperate need for believers everywhere to become fully alive in the realm of love—that they might be fully prepared for the culminating events before Christ's return.

THE INTERNATIONAL HOUSE OF PRAYER OF KANSAS CITY

On September 19, 1999, a prayer and worship meeting began in South Kansas City that continues to this very hour. For over four years, night-and-day worship with intercession has gone up before the throne of God. The International House of Prayer of Kansas City is a 24-hour, citywide, inter-denominational prayer ministry that is modeled after the Tabernacle of David (1 Chr. 13-16; 23-25.) and focused on the "prayer side" of the Great Commission. It is based on the reality that worship, music and intercession flow together in heaven around God's Throne (Rev. 4-5). The Scripture prophesies that God will again raise up the Tabernacle of David in the context of gathering the Great Harvest of new believers at the end of the age (Acts 15:16; Amos 9:11). This implies a dynamic worldwide "intercessory worship" movement that will be in full force during the generation in which the Lord returns.

Convinced that Jesus is worthy of incessant adoration, men and women of all ages from across the globe are giving themselves to extravagant love expressed through 24/7 prayer and worship. Structured in eighty-four two-hour meetings a week, full teams of musicians, singers, and intercessors (missionaries) lift their voices in praise and supplication, asking God to fulfill His promise and give the nations of the earth to Jesus as His inheritance.

For more info on the International House of Prayer of Kansas City visit: www.fotb.com.